KT-432-045

the **information** store
📞01603 773114
email: tis@ccn.?

For David, ... and Belinda

Acknowledgements

Lots of people have helped in the writing of this Pocket Essential. Firstly I would like to thank Antony Coulson and Marieke Krajenbrink for providing me with copies of some of the harder to get films. Also I would like to thank Belinda Brindle, Jonathan Grix, Alison Fell, Mikel Koven and Rob Stone for reading and commenting on parts of the manuscript. Also thanks to Wini Davies. Finally I'd like to thank the students on my Weimar Cinema course whose enthusiastic contributions in class have had a big influence on my readings of many of the films discussed here.

204 238

Paul Cooke

The Pocket Essential

GERMAN EXPRESSIONIST FILMS

www.pocketessentials.com

First published in Great Britain 2002 by Pocket Essentials,
18 Coleswood Road, Harpenden, Herts, AL5 1EQ

Distributed in the USA by Trafalgar Square Publishing, PO Box 257,
Howe Hill Road, North Pomfret, Vermont 05053

Copyright © Paul Cooke 2002
Series Editor: Paul Duncan

The right of Paul Cooke to be identified as the author of this work has been asserted
by him in accordance with the Copyright, Designs and Patents Act 1988.

All rights reserved. No part of this book may be reproduced, stored in or introduced
into a retrieval system, or transmitted, in any form, or by any means (electronic,
mechanical, photocopying, recording or otherwise) without the written permission of
the publisher.
Any person who does any unauthorised act in relation to this publication may be lia-
ble to criminal prosecution and civil claims for damages. The book is sold subject to
the condition that it shall not, by way of trade or otherwise, be lent, re-sold, hired out
or otherwise circulated, without the publisher's prior consent, in any form or binding
or cover other than in which it is published, and without similar conditions, including
this condition being imposed on the subsequent publication.

A CIP catalogue record for this book is available from the British Library.

ISBN 1-904048-01-3

2 4 6 8 10 9 7 5 3 1

Book typeset by Wordsmith Solutions Ltd
Printed and bound by Cox & Wyman

CONTENTS

204238
791.430943 Coo

NORWICH CITY COLLEGE
LIBRARY

Introduction

So why read about German Expressionist film, those strange early German movies, full of weird sets, exaggerated acting and curious camera angles? Well, plenty of people would tell you not to bother. Mainstream audiences don't normally flock to see the rare showings of these movies. Rob (John Cusack) in Stephen Frears' *High Fidelity* (2000) seems to say it all when he lists one of his top five jobs as "film director - any type apart from silent or German." In German Expressionism you've got both. I can sometimes see the blood drain from the faces of the students on my film course when they realise what they've let themselves in for, and now you're probably thinking of putting this back on the shelf and picking up the Pocket Essential *Steven Spielberg* or *Blaxploitation Films*.

If I haven't totally put you off, here are some answers to the question. The first reason has to be because of the massive influence German Expressionism has had on subsequent generations of film-makers. From *Frankenstein* (1931) to *Blade Runner* (1982), *The Wizard Of Oz* (1939) to *Batman* (1989), it's touched them all. And it's not just important when looking at feature films. Expressionism is also regularly plundered by pop stars, with bands and artists like Queen, Yahoo and Madonna ripping off films from this period for their videos, revealing the extent to which it remains important for contemporary popular consciousness. Secondly, the film culture of which German Expressionism was part was a springboard for some of the most important figures in twentieth-century film history. It was during this golden age of German cinema that Alfred Hitchcock got his first break, directing his first feature film *The Pleasure Garden* in Munich in 1925, and where Fritz Lang started out before making it in Hollywood. If you really want to get a thorough picture of what influenced American film, certainly in the first half of the twentieth century, this is the place to start looking.

The era of German Expressionist film is normally thought to start in the aftermath of World War One and go up to the mid-1920s - coinciding with the silent movie period. In this book, we're going to broaden that out a bit, looking also at the effect the movement had on later films. However, before we can get into talking about this, we need to fill in a bit of background, looking at what was around before Expressionism really got going and what it was influenced by. In the European cinema stakes, Germany got off to a relatively late start. Although the first moving pictures were exhibited in Germany at the same time as the Lumière Brothers were setting up in France, German cinema didn't really take off until the second decade of the twentieth century. This was due in no small part to the cultural snobbery of a lot of the German intelligentsia. Film was seen as a refuge for the uneducated and the immoral, a reputation which becomes more understandable when you look at the films that were being shown. In the makeshift tent cinemas and nickelodeons that were springing up around the country, audiences were treated either to foreign imports or a feast of simplistic German-made shorts. The subject matter of these shorts was very diverse. They might be about fairground freaks or show views of some of Germany's major cities. However a good deal of them were pornographic in nature, giving the spectator tantalising glimpses of, for example, luscious ladies taking baths. No wonder the high-minded intelligentsia, as well as the rest of the German bourgeoisie, considered film (officially at least) beneath them.

Slowly things began to change. This happened, on the one hand, through the efforts of film entrepreneurs like Oskar Messter (who set up some of the first proper film studios in Germany) and, on the other, through the influence of the *film d'art* movement in France, which was treating this new medium as a serious art form. In the years leading up to World War One there was a noticeable shift in attitude, discernible particularly in the fact that some of the big names of the German highbrow culture were beginning to get involved with film. Major writers such as Gerhart Hauptmann and Hugo von Hofmannsthal were beginning to publicly endorse the cinema by producing screenplays. Many others were far more hypocritical, being privately happy to take a film company's cash by writing for it, while publicly continuing to attack the cinema as vulgar and philistine. Apart from famous writers, the big stars of the theatre also made the transition to film, most notably the director and producer Max Reinhardt. What was particularly important about Reinhardt, however, was not just the films he made, such as *Die Insel der Seligen/The Isle Of The Dead* (1913). More significantly, Reinhardt's theatre troupe became a seedbed of talent for the German film industry, providing many of its key figures in the 1920s, including Ernst Lubitsch (who was the first in a long line of German directors to be poached by Hollywood, where he went on to become the king of the screwball comedy in the 1930s) and Paul Wegener, who co-directed some of the best early films, including *Der Student von Prag/The Student Of Prague* (1913) and *Der Golem/The Golem* (1914), both of which were remade in the 1920s.

It is in films like these that we see the beginnings of German Expressionism and the shift to what became known as *Autorenfilm*, a term usually thought to have been invented by critics in the 1950s and 1960s associated with the French New Wave, who talked about *auteur* films. However, whilst the French critics used the term to differentiate films which bore the thumbprint of a specific film-maker, *Autorenfilm* were generally defined by their screenplay writers, artists who where beginning to produce scenarios which differed markedly from the generic set pieces which had been churned out until then. The film credited with being the first *Autorenfilm* is *Der Andere/The Other* by Max Mack. Made in 1913, *Der Andere* is a Jekyll and Hyde story about a Berlin lawyer, Dr Hallers, who falls into a deep sleep after an accident, only to wake and find that he now has an evil double. However, this was a watershed moment in German film not only due to the fact that Mack can be seen as the first *Autor*, but also because it starred the world famous stage actor Albert Bassermann, thereby moving film up another notch in the respectability stakes. Also, as the film critic Wolfgang Jacobsen points out, it is in this film that you can really begin to see elements of the Expressionist style, particularly in Bassermann's acting, which would play a major role in German film after the war.

The War And Ufa

The German film industry really took off during World War One. Starved of its normal supply of British, French and US imports, the indigenous industry had to crank up production to fulfil the public's growing hunger for movies. The turnaround in the fortunes of German films was incredible, with production by 1918 up 1000% on its pre-War levels. The films produced, however, varied in quality. There was, of course, a good deal of nationalistic propaganda made. But as the film critic Thomas Elsaesser notes, not all the films that dealt with the War and other social issues at the time can be dismissed in this way. He points, for example, to the excellent *Das Tagebuch des Dr Hart/The Diary Of Dr Hart* (1916), which tells the moving story of two families divided by differing political loyalties. This film was the directing debut of Paul Leni, another important figure in the story of Expressionism, who would go on to make *Wachsfigurenkabinett/Waxworks* (1924) - a key film of the period. As well as Leni, several other important post-war figures now began to rise to fame. This is when Ernst Lubitsch started to work and when the producer Eric Pommer - one of the main driving forces of Expressionism - entered the scene, setting up his film company Deola. This is the company that would eventually produce the first 'real' Expressionist film, *Das Cabinet des Dr Caligari/The Cabinet Of Dr Caligari* after the War in 1919. Another important development at this time for our story is the rise of the fantastic or fairy-tale film. What began before the War with Wegener and *Der Student von Prag* (1913) continued with films such as Otto Rippert's six-part *Homunculus* (1916). In these movies film-makers draw on the dark nineteenth-century Romantic tradition of writers such as E.T.A. Hoffmann as well as German and Jewish folklore to produce disturbing mythical landscapes, landscapes which after the war would evolve into the Expressionistic nightmares of films by Wiene, Lang and Murnau.

But probably the single most important event for post-war film-making in Germany that took place during the conflict was the creation of the film company Ufa (Universum Film Aktiengesellschaft) in December of 1917. Fearful that the German film industry wasn't doing its bit to win the hearts and minds of the German people for the War effort, the commander-in-chief of the army, Erich Ludendorff, brought together a conglomerate of bankers, industrialists and representatives of the army to form a massive national film company. The economic clout of Ufa was huge. As a result it was able to expand voraciously both vertically (buying up distribution companies and cinemas) and horizontally (taking over most of the major production companies, with the notable exception of Eric Pommer's Decla, which held out until 1921). Amid the chaos of the aftermath of the War this company went from strength to strength, a development which might seem rather surprising when you think about what was happening in the rest of the country at the time.

The Weimar Republic: Streetfighting And Movie-Going

Like most other European countries, the German population was decimated by the War. Of the 11 million men called up, over 7 million were either killed, injured or missing. But unlike Britain or France, Germany's political system was also wiped out. For the first time in its history the country rejected an authoritarian monarchy, replacing it with a parliamentary democracy. This had a huge altering effect on people, bringing with it, on the one hand, a great sense of intellectual liberation - for example, the censorship of the previous administration was abolished and women were given the vote. But, on the other, working against this sense of liberation from the past was the strong feeling that democracy was an inherently unstable system. At its very birth it looked like this new democracy could be wiped out, since the republic was set up at a time when Berlin found itself in the grip of a Russian-style Communist revolution. This meant the government had to flee Berlin and hold its first assembly in the town of Weimar (hence this period of German history being called the Weimar Republic). The revolution was quickly put down by right-wing paramilitary groups of demobbed soldiers, who then proceeded to try to take over the state themselves. Eventually, order was restored, and the government could get on with organising itself, but a dangerous precedent was set. Democracy was seen as weak, a perception which led many people to believe in direct action. This made the cities of Weimar Germany pretty dangerous places to live, with left- and right-wing thugs regularly clashing on the streets.

If the Weimar Republic was politically unstable, its economy was in no better shape. The costs of the War, coupled with the massive amount of money the Allies were demanding in reparations, brought the country to its knees and lead to a period of hyperinflation that, at its height in 1923, saw a Dollar valued at 4.2 billion Marks. By the time you'd put your wages into your pocket they'd lost value, and people were forced into the ludicrous situation of, for example, carrying wheelbarrows of money to the bakers, just to buy a loaf of bread. Eventually the Mark stabilised, but a lot of people lost everything as they saw their bank savings reduced to nothing.

Yet, strangely the very conditions that were wrecking most other parts of German society were precisely the reasons why the film industry did so well. Firstly, the economic situation meant that foreign companies didn't want to import films, because German money wasn't worth anything. As a result the market was clear for home-grown products. Secondly, hyperinflation meant that the value of money borrowed to make films in Germany evaporated, so they could be produced very cheaply. If, for example, a company borrowed 50,000DM in January to make a film, by September, when they had finished the film and had to pay the money back it would be worthless. Thirdly, people felt that there was little point in saving, since money would just lose its value anyway, consequently the amount of people's income that was treated as disposable increased. Fourthly, Ufa, being a massive company, had a lot of money invested in property such as the huge Neubabelsberg Studio near Berlin. Investment in property, unlike bank savings, was inflation proof. And finally, the film industry flourished because in a time when society is going through a period of massive social and political upheaval the escapism of the movies provides great relief.

Although Ufa was set up as a military structure, the bankers and industrialists involved were far more interested in commercial success, which limited any simplistic propagandist agenda that Ludendorff might originally have had. It was they who held the purse strings and by the early 1920s, when it finally merged with Decla and came under the control of Erich Pommer, it was indeed a financial success and could even compete with the Hollywood studio system on which it modelled itself. Through its programme of mergers, a huge amount of talent came under its umbrella, major stars such as Asta Nielsen, Pola Negri and Emil Jannings along with directors such as Lubitsch, Lang, Robert Wiene, F.W. Murnau and G.W. Pabst. But not only could Ufa copy the organisation of Hollywood, due to the amount of money at its disposal, its stars could also start to demand salaries equivalent to those being paid in Hollywood, helping, for a time, to keep them working in Germany.

In terms of the films being made by Ufa (and before the merger by Decla), it is possible to identify a number of broad trends. You had exotic adventure films like Fritz Lang's *Die Spinnen/The Spiders* (1919), or you had big costume dramas like Ernst Lubitsch's *Madame Dubarry* (1919) (one of the first films to put German cinema on the map in America). There was also the *Kammerspielfilm* (*Chamber-drama film*), like Lupu Pick's *Sylvester/New Year's Eve* (1923), or Murnau's *Der letzte Mann/The Last Laugh* (1924). Finally, there were Expressionist films and until 1927 it was this type of film-making that was the real flagship of German cinema abroad (although it's important to remember that they didn't dominate the domestic German film market). It's these films, as well as the films that came afterwards and were influenced by them, the films of so-called *Neue Sachlichkeit* or *New Objectivity*, with which we're most concerned here, and to which I shall return shortly.

In the early 1920s then, Germany could compete with Hollywood and was particularly dominant in Europe. But that's not to say that Hollywood didn't remain an important force. First of all, the Hollywood system was the model that Ufa, to a degree, emulated, culminating in Pommer and Lang being sent over to the States to learn directly from the masters and to set up links. This trip had important consequences for film history in more ways than one, since it was from his first view of New York that Lang got the idea for the city in *Metropolis*. As the 1920s went on, however, it became increasingly hard for Weimar to compete with the US. More and more stars and directors were being lured away to Hollywood as the conditions in America began to outstrip those in Germany. Also, an increasing percentage of the Germany industry was funded by the big American companies. This was accelerated in the mid-1920s because Ufa was nearly bankrupted by the production costs of *Metropolis*. With a stable economy, real debts had to be paid for with real money that Ufa didn't have. Paramount stepped in and the company was saved. But the writing was on the wall for the German film industry, which went into a slow decline until it was finally taken over by the Nazis in 1933.

What Is Expressionism?

We now come to the question of aesthetics, and the problem of defining the term Expressionism. German Expressionism is the term used to describe a cultural movement which started up in Germany at the beginning of the twentieth century. This was a time when the pace of change in society throughout Europe really began to take off. The speed of industrial change was accelerating, bringing more and more people into the cities that were also quickly growing in size. Radio and film technology was making the world a more accessible place. Einstein was discovering his theory of relativity, and so reinventing physics. Freud was challenging the way we thought individuals functioned with his theories of the unconscious mind; and the philosophy of Nietzsche, who had declared the 'Death of God,' was ushering in a new 'post-Christian' era of thought. In response to the new reality all these changes were producing, the Expressionists attempted to find a new way of representing the world in art and literature. They rejected the nineteenth-century aesthetics of 'realism' and 'naturalism,' which attempted to give objective snapshots of reality, claiming that such schools of art only gave a partial picture - one fifth of the iceberg above the water, if you like. What the Expressionists wanted to show was the other four fifths, that part of the world which lies beneath the visible, beyond the knowable. Rather than giving simply an objective view of the world, they wanted to explore the individual's subjective psychological reaction to this new and rapidly changing society.

Groups of painters such as *Die Blaue Reiter* in Munich and *Die Brücke* in Dresden experimented with stark, crudely abstract images and vivid colours in their quest to represent this new reality. Elsewhere, poets and dramatists played with language to find a new linguistic logic, to discover a new means of making sense of this ever-changing reality. The actual images of the world that the Expressionists produced varied greatly, but taken together they communicate an overwhelming feeling of ambivalence to society, perhaps best summed up in the title of a famous anthology of Expressionist poetry by Kurt Pinthus, *Menschheitsdämmerung/Twilight of Humanity* (1920). The ambiguity of the term 'twilight' is the key here. Were these people living at the dawn of a new age, full of hope and promise, or were they really just witnessing the death and destruction of the old one, with no hope of a new beginning? Throughout these poems you can hear the desperate Expressionist scream of 'O Mensch!' (Oh Humanity!), an exclamation of the Expressionist artists' perception that they were being psychologically torn apart by the simultaneous senses of fear and wonder they felt.

And How Does It Relate To Film?

Curiously, if you had asked a lot of the film-makers under discussion here whether they were Expressionists they'd probably have asked you to step outside. Fritz Lang in particular always denied the films that he made had anything to do with this movement. The films that are considered to be Expressionist differ wildly, with some critics claiming that there are as little as half a dozen truly Expressionist films, while others see the term as largely synonymous with the whole of Weimar Cinema.

That Expressionism was so attractive to post-war film-makers was not surprising. After the War, the forces of modernity didn't look like they were slowing down, and the sense of ambiguity felt by artists did nothing but increase. Firstly, as we've already seen, the social upheavals that were beginning before the War went into overdrive during the Weimar period. Also, the pace of technological change was now even more problematic than before. On the one hand, the movies and radio were continuing to shrink the world, giving people access to places they could have only ever dreamt of before, but this same progress also brought them the tank and the machine gun, weapons of mass destruction used so effectively on the battlefields of the Western Front. So how do such ambiguities manifest themselves in film?

Most commonly, critics trying to define Expressionist film tend to focus on certain aspects of film style, the most important of these being the use of a flat, theatrical *mise en scène* that attempted to copy the distorted, abstract style of the Expressionist painters of *Die Brücke* and *Die Blaue Reiter*. This is an aspect which particularly came to the fore with Wiene's *Caligari*. Lighting is also considered to be central to Expressionist film style. In particular the use of 'chiaroscuro,' or extremes of light and shadow, which produce frames full of contrast. These effects were then coupled with a highly stylised form of acting, designed to match the abstraction of the *mise en scène*. Characters were larger than life, their exaggerated facial expressions being an attempt to communicate the inner, psychological dimensions of the character, thereby undermining simplistic realism. Finally, the editing and camerawork tended (at least early on) to be quite simple, relying mainly on shot/reverse shot and cross-cutting to maintain continuity. If we take all these traits to be necessary for a film to be considered Expressionist then we don't find very many that fit the bill. The critic Barry Salt suggests that you can only identify six, and certainly you don't see many purely Expressionist films beyond 1924. This is not surprising of course, since good film-makers will normally try and find new ways of expressing their ideas. So, once the 'rules' of Expressionist *mise en scène*, acting and editing had become established, the very people that helped form them proceeded to break them. However, if we include those films that were highly influenced by Expressionism the number we have to choose from increases greatly. In this oeuvre, it's not just film style that becomes important, but also the themes explored by pre-war Expressionist artists.

The problem of the pace of change, coupled with a wish to convey the inner psychological world of the individual, was a major preoccupation of film-makers of the time. In the work of directors like Lang and Wiene we find a strong feeling that humanity is being taken over and destroyed by technology, as people are reduced to the level of automated drones in the production lines of capitalism. This in turn led many of the film-makers we are going to look at, such as Wegener, to question the nature of cinema and the mass media. Was this new technology simply bringing people together to liberate them, or was it a dangerous form of mind control that would lead to society's destruction?

As well as the question of the role of technology in society, the notion of exploring those unconscious desires and fears that Freud claimed we try to lock away in our subconscious remained an important focus for film-makers, right up to the rise of the Nazis. These desires and fears were defined in Freud's work by the two Greek gods Eros and Thanatos, figures he used to denote the sex and death drives that, Freud claimed, are to be found at the heart of every individual. In the early period this impulse to explore the unconscious can be seen in directors' predilection for horrific fantasy stories. However, even in the films of the *New Objectivity* that came after the first flush of Expressionism, such as those made by G.W. Pabst, and which have a much more realist edge to them, we can still see the aftershocks of this earlier phase. Thus, if we take this broader approach we can even include films such as von Sternberg's *Der Blaue Engel* (*The Blue Angel*) (1930) in a study of Expressionism.

Approaches to Expressionism and to Weimar Cinema in general have been largely influenced by two books, Siegfried Kracauer's *From Caligari To Hitler: A Psychological History Of German Film* (1947) and Lotte Eisner's *The Haunted Screen: Expressionism In The German Cinema And The Influence Of Max Reinhardt* (1952). Both these books were produced by German exiles in the aftermath of the Second World War and used film to explain the catastrophic takeover of Germany by the Nazis. In Kracauer's study, he selectively reads the first decades of German film history to show how the authoritarian traits later to be found in National Socialism could be observed on the big screen of the 1920s. Kracauer's book has been criticised over the years for only selecting those films which back up his argument rather than giving an objective picture, but it still remains a very important work for people interested in the period. Eisner's main focus, on the other hand, is the question of influence; that is, she looks at the various artistic movements which shaped the period. Eisner uses a broad definition of the term Expressionism, not really differentiating it from other artistic movements such as Romanticism. Like Kracauer, Eisner reads these films in terms of their social context but she emphasises the style of the films over the content. Despite her different approach, she too concludes that the crisis at the heart of the German national consciousness is plain to see in Weimar Cinema.

More recently, Thomas Elsaesser has challenged these views. He notes, for example, that there were lots of factors influencing film at the time, not just Expressionism, and far from manifesting a disturbed German soul, the films occasionally parody earlier traditions. More importantly he looks at film institutions, highlighting the role of marketing in the adoption of the term Expressionism. He explains, for example, how Pommer deliberately used the concept of Expressionism as a 'brand name' to market *Caligari* abroad. In so doing he hoped to overcome prejudice against German products by constructing it as an art-house film, and therefore worthy of an audience. Then, when German film-makers began to flee the Nazis Elsaesser claims that they used this brand name as a form of cultural capital: 'It advertised their creativity and their professionalism, but also their adaptability and survival skills, which the Hollywood dream factory made good use of.' The influence of German film style has particularly been noted on the Hollywood Film Noir of the 1940s and 1950s.

In my overview of Expressionist film I aim to steer a path through all these readings. I look at how Expressionism manifested itself in both the style and the content of German films from the beginning of the *Autorenfilm* through to the 1930s. Firstly I look at the first flush of the movement, giving you a taste of some early fantasy/horror films, before looking in detail at three key directors - Fritz Lang, F.W. Murnau and G.W. Pabst. Finally I go on to explore how Expressionism continued to play a role after its heyday, looking at its influence on certain talkies. Here I also show the role played in cinema by figures from the literary avant-garde of which the 'real' Expressionist movement was a part - in particular the poet and dramatist Bertold Brecht.

1. Monsters, Doppelgänger And Madmen: The First Flush Of Expressionism

This chapter looks at some of the key films that kicked off Expressionism, from the pre-war period through to its heyday in the early 1920s. Clearly it would be impossible to write about all the films, but the four I've chosen give a flavour of the style and content of 'classic' Expressionist film. The filmography at the back of this book has a long list of German Expressionist films for you to investigate.

Der Student von Prag/The Student Of Prague (1913)

Cast: Grete Berger (Komtesse Margit), John Gottowt (Scapinelli), Lothar Körner (Baron von Schwarzenberg), Lyda Salmonova (Lyduschka), Paul Wegener (Balduin and Second Balduin), Fritz Weidemann (Baron Waldis-Schwarzenberg)

Crew: Directors Stellan Rye and Paul Wegener, Writer Hanns Heinz Ewers and Paul Wegener, Cinematography Guido Seeber, Production Design Robert A. Deitrich and Kurt Richter, Deutsche Bioscop

Story: In nineteenth-century Prague, the student Balduin is not faring too well, his wild nights of drunken debauchery having left him crippled by debt. Enter Scapinelli, the mysterious evil sorcerer, who listens to Balduin's tale of woe and his longing for riches and a wealthy wife, a desire which greatly upsets gypsy girl Lyduschka who has a soft spot for our hero.

At a hunt, the beautiful aristocrat Komtesse Margit is being wooed by Baron von Schwarzenberg. She is appalled by the Baron's advances, and even more appalled to learn that her family want her to marry him. She tells the nobleman that although she will ultimately accept the will of her family, she will never love him, and rides off in disgust. In her dismay she loses control of her horse and is thrown into a lake. Luckily, who should be walking past but the student Balduin. He heroically dives in and saves her, then falls madly in love with her. Margit's father invites Balduin to his palace to thank him properly. Unfortunately he turns up at the same time as the Baron. Clearly he can't compete with his rival's riches so he withdraws to his garret to wallow in self-pity.

Re-enter Scapinelli, who has a deal for Balduin, He will sort out the student's money problems and so give him a chance with the Komtesse. All he asks in return is to be allowed to take anything he wants from Balduin's room. The poor student has nothing of any value so he agrees. But, once Balduin signs the pact the devious Scapinelli reveals his intention. In return for the money he wants Balduin's reflection, which the evil sorcerer then proceeds to draw out of the mirror in his room. Balduin is initially rather perturbed but soon forgets about his pact as his thoughts return to the money he now has. The next thing we see is Balduin courting the Komtesse and living it up in high society.

However, Balduin soon realises his problems aren't over. He begins to be plagued by his reflection which appears as a disturbing Doppelgänger every time he starts to get close to Margit. Meanwhile, Lyduschka is also stirring up trouble. Jealous of his relationship with the Komtesse, she tries to spoil Balduin's chances by letting her fiancé know that he has a rival. Inevitably, the Baron challenges Balduin to a duel. Since Balduin is widely known to be the best fencer in town, Margit's father asks him to go easy on the Baron. This he promises to do, but on the appointed day he is deliberately delayed by Scapinelli, and when he finally arrives at the duel he is met by his double who is holding a bloody sword. The Doppelgänger has murdered the Baron.

Balduin then goes to the Komtesse's house to protest his innocence but nobody is interested in talking to him, so he decides to find solace in a night of gambling and drinking. At his club he meets his double again who tries to make Balduin take the ultimate gamble - his own life against the life of his reflection. Balduin attempts to flee but ultimately cannot escape, finally understanding that he must kill his double to be free. He grabs his pistol and shoots his reflection, only to realise too late that he has shot himself. As he lies dead on the floor of his room, Scapinelli returns. Laughing grotesquely, the sorcerer tears up the contract he had with the student and sprinkles the pieces on his corpse. Finally, we cut to Balduin's grave, where we see that the evil double is still alive, eerily keeping watch over his dead alter ego.

Background: If *Caligari* is the father of Expressionism, *Der Student von Prag* can be seen as the father of *Caligari*. This film and others like *Der Andere* (1913) is generally seen to be amongst the first *Autorenfilm* in Germany. It was a huge success, shooting its star and co-director Paul Wegener into the limelight. Technically it's very crude, relying primarily on a static camera and long takes. The film is driven completely by the actors' performances. As a result, there's a very theatrical feel to a lot of the film, a feel which seems to be deliberately foregrounded in the title sequence, during which each of the main characters appears on a stage from behind a curtain. That said, there are one or two interesting camera tricks. Particularly impressive is the sequence in which the doppelgänger steps out from the mirror to the shock and amazement of Balduin. In terms of *mise en scène* there is very little that is Expressionistic about this film. It is mainly shot using natural light and on location on the streets of Prague. As Lotte Eisner suggests, 'the Expressionist style which had been the ruling taste in all the other arts since 1910 had not as yet got through to the cinema, which was still regarded with scorn.' Consequently we see none of the distorted landscapes and abstract acting that was to become the vogue after the war. Interestingly, in 1926 the film was remade, and this time it was completely derivative of *Caligari*, replacing the external scenes of this film with internal, artificial images. However, whilst the form of the film might not be very Expressionistic, its content and subtext certainly prefigure what was to come.

Subtext: The story comes from a number of sources, from *Faust*, to E.T.A. Hoffmann to Edgar Allan Poe. Poe and Hoffmann in particular show the influence of nineteenth-century literary tradition on early German film. The main theme of the film is the nature of the human psyche, a theme which was to become central to German cinema after the War. Balduin's double embodies his unconscious desires, those irrational urges, the sex and death drives that Freud claimed we keep locked away deep within ourselves, away from rational society. Every time Balduin attempts to woo his lady, his double appears, signifying to the spectator the student's true lustful intentions. The doubling of Balduin is then also mirrored in the two women in the film, the Komtesse and the gypsy Lyduschka. Here you have the classic Virgin/Whore split found in representations of women throughout the literature of the nineteenth century. The women are simply external projections of Balduin's internal crisis, Margit symbolising his desire for integration into the rational respectability of Prague society life, a wish that is undermined by Lyduschka, who symbolises his irrational desires that refuse to remain quiet. The good/bad split is then also symbolised in the opposition

21

in the film between 'rational' Christianity (again symbolised in the Komtesse, who in one sequence looks for guidance from the church) and 'irrational' Judaism. Scapinelli the evil sorcerer is decidedly Semitic looking. Also,
when Balduin sets up a tryst with the Komtesse where should he choose to
meet her but in a Jewish graveyard, thus bringing together most clearly his
death and sex drives unlocked by his pact with Scapinelli.

Verdict: This is an interesting film, and well worth a watch. The only
drawbacks are firstly its technical limitations (although these are generally
balanced out by Guido Seeber's flashes of imagination in his camerawork,
particularly in the sequences where we see the double) and secondly its
dodgy anti-Semitic undertones. 3/5

Das Cabinet des Doktor Caligari/
The Cabinet Of Doctor Caligari (1920)

Cast: Werner Krauss (Dr Caligari), Conrad Veidt (Cesare), Friedrich
Feher (Francis), Lil Dagover (Jane), Hans von Twardowski (Alan), Rudolf
Lettinger (Dr Olson), Rudolf Klein-Rogge (The Criminal)

Crew: Director Robert Wiene, Writers Hans Janowitz and Carl Mayer,
Producer Erich Pommer, Cinematography Willi Hameister, Production
Design Hermann Warm, Walter Röhrig and Walter Reimann, Decla

Story: Francis tells his companion of the frightening events that happened to both him and his fiancée Jane, the ghostly figure passing by the
two men in a trance-like state…

Francis' home town of Holstenwall is in the grip of a serial killer. The
timing of the murders committed by this killer have also coincided with the
arrival of a travelling fair, at which we meet the mysterious Dr Caligari, a
freak show stallholder at the fair, who exhibits the hypnotised somnambulist
Cesare. Kept by day in a coffin-like cabinet, Cesare is woken by Caligari at
the show to predict the future of members of the audience. Alan, Francis'
best friend and rival for the love of Jane, asks Cesare to tell him how long he
will live. "Until dawn," comes the ominous reply. The next day Alan is
found dead and Cesare becomes the main suspect.

Francis begins a vigil to watch Cesare while he sleeps in his cabinet but
little does Francis know that he is watching a dummy and Cesare has crept
into Jane's bedroom with the intention of killing her. As the somnambulist

looks at her he realises that he can't go through with it, so instead he abducts the girl, kicking and screaming, from her bedroom. A chase follows. Jane is saved but Cesare escapes (only later to be found dead). Francis confronts Caligari and discovers that he has been tricked. In the ensuing chaos the doctor escapes. Another chase takes place, during which Caligari takes refuge in a lunatic asylum.

When Francis arrives at the asylum, he is shocked to find that Caligari is its director and as the director sleeps Francis learns the truth about the man from his journal. The director had become obsessed with an eighteenth-century showman named Caligari, who travelled through Italy using a hypnotised man to kill people. When Cesare turned up as a patient the director saw it as an opportunity to fulfil his dream of following in Caligari's footsteps. Having established the truth, Francis and the nurses in the asylum bind the director up in a straitjacket and lock him in a cell.

The film then flashes forward to Francis and his companion as we saw them at the start. The director, we are told, is still locked in his cell. But then, as Francis goes with his companion back to the asylum, we see some of the figures in his story, among them Cesare, who is now apparently alive. The truth slowly dawns that Francis is an inmate in the asylum and that it is he, and not the director, who is the madman. The director appears amongst the patients and Francis loses control, screaming that the man is Caligari. Now it is Francis' turn to be locked up in a cell. But, in the final shot there seems to be a glimmer of hope. The camera focuses in on the director who calmly assures us that now he knows the cause of Francis' lunacy he can at last cure him.

Background: This is the film that really started the Expressionist movement, taking German film from the realms of cheap entertainment to high art. It also helped to put the horror/fantasy film at the centre of this high art end of the Weimar film market, inspiring on its release in France the craze of 'Caligarisme.' Particularly influential on subsequent films was the *mise en scène*, designed by Expressionist artists Hermann Warm, Walter Röhrig and Walter Reimann. All three men belonged to the Expressionist *Sturm* group and famously declared that the best films were not simply photo-like representations of reality, but rather 'drawings brought to life.' The world of the film looks just like an Expressionist painting in which jagged, out of perspective buildings jut out at strange angles from the landscape. There's a very oppressive feel to the film, a feeling that is compounded by the fact that all the lighting effects are just painted on the scenery, making the whole thing seem very theatrical. The non-realist, staged nature of the film is then further emphasised by the larger-than-life, stylised performances of Werner Krauss, who is breathtaking as the sinister Caligari, and of Conrad Veidt as Cesare. Both actors would go on to figure in many major German, and in Veidt's case American, movies. (Veidt later turned up as Major Strasser in *Casablanca* (1942).)

The ending of the film, that is when we realise that the story has been made up by Francis using characters from his surroundings, has been copied by film-makers as diverse as Victor Fleming in *The Wizard Of Oz* (1939) and Bryan Singer in *The Usual Suspects* (1995). In *Caligari* it was an ending that caused a good degree of controversy. According to Kracauer, when Janowitz and Mayer first gave the script to Erich Pommer it was without the flashback framing device. These men, who had lived through the horrors of the First World War, conceived of the film as the story of authoritarian power (embodied in director of the asylum) gone mad. Pommer then gave the script to Lang to film, but Lang was worried about the film's message, so he wrote the framing sequences, which turned the whole story into the rantings of a madman. The director is confirmed as a goody and society's authority figure is left unquestioned. In the end Lang was replaced by Wiene so that Lang could go off and film the second part of *Die Spinnen/ The Spiders* (1920), but the frame sequences were kept, much to the annoyance of Janowitz who felt it totally undermined his original intention. Kracauer got this version of story from Janowitz. However, since telling it in his book *From Caligari to Hitler* it has been denied by a number of people, not least by Lang who was furious with Kracauer for including it. There is, as Thomas Elsaesser notes, a large degree of doubt about who put in the frame, with some people suggesting that it might have been either Wiene or Janowitz's co-writer Carl Mayer.

Subtext: Arguments about the framing device don't end with who wrote it. The jury is also still out on whether, as Kracauer claims, it turns a controversial, disturbing film into a cosy isn't-society-wonderful-we-can-cure-the-sick story. The main problems with Kracauer's version is that the frame doesn't answer all our questions. Firstly, as the critic Richard Murphy points out, when the film starts, we think we're going to get the story of

Francis and Jane, but in the end we don't. This relationship is only mentioned in passing as the film turns into the search for Alan's murderer. The film promises a story it never delivers. Secondly, if the end really is nothing but an hallucination by Francis, why are some of the key figures in his story, most notably Alan, missing from the asylum? In *The Wizard Of Oz* everyone's there. Finally, if the main story is an Expressionistic representation of Francis' troubled mind, why is the same *mise en scène* used in the framing device? It's as if the frame can't hold the main story in check, a fact which causes us to feel very uncomfortable in the final sequence where Francis is locked up and the director claims that he can 'cure' him. Who really is the madman?

Again, as we saw in *Der Student von Prag*, the nature of desire plays an important thematic role in the film, neatly communicated by the character (or rather lack of character) of Cesare. Many commentators see Cesare as the fulfiller of the characters' subconscious wishes. As Elsaesser points out, this works because the story makes sense from a variety of perspectives, with Cesare acting as an empty symbol who can be assigned different meanings according to the angle from which the film is approached. For example, while, on one level, Cesare might be seen as a monster who carries out the bidding of his unhinged master, he could also be seen as an externalisation of Francis' subconscious desire to destroy his rival, Alan, and to carry off Jane, his bride to be.

Another theme in the film is the relation of cinema itself to society. This is most clearly shown in the sequence where we first meet Cesare. The camera follows the crowds into Caligari's tent, placing the film's spectator in the audience of the freak show. Then, we slowly move to the front of the audience where we watch Cesare wake. When he finally opens his eyes the monster is shocked at the sight of the audience, but at this point the only audience we can see is the one in the cinema of which we are a part. Cesare looks with horror directly at us, reversing the normal relationship between the spectator and the film and jarring us out of our passive acceptance of the pictures flickering on the screen. For a moment the dream-world of the film cracks and there is a real person staring at us, shocked by the fact that we have been staring at him, thus forcing us to think about why we are watching the film.

Verdict: The importance of this film for future generations, just like so many from the period, can't be underestimated. This alone would give it full marks. The stylised performances and *mise en scène* might seem a bit clichéd at times (a result in part at least of the fact that the film has provided a model for so many others) but it still has the power to grip audiences. 5/5

Der Golem, wie er in die Welt kam/
The Golem: How He Came Into The World (1920)

Cast: Paul Wegener (The Golem), Albert Steinrück (Rabbi Loew), Lyda Salmonova (Miriam), Ernst Deutsch (Famulus), Hans Stürm (Rabbi Jehuda), Max Kronert (Temple Servant), Otto Gebühr (Emperor Luhois), Lothar Müthel (Florian), Greta Schröder (Little Girl)

Crew: Directors Paul Wegener and Carl Boese, Writers Henrik Galeen and Paul Wegener, Producer Paul Davison, Cinematography Karl Freund, Production Design Hans Poelzig and Kurt Richter, Projektion-AG Union

Story: In sixteenth-century Prague the Jewish ghetto is under attack by the Emperor Luhois who wants to kick the Jews out of his city. To save his people Rabbi Loew, a powerful mystic, creates the Golem, a clay figure that he brings to life by invoking the evil spirit Astaroth. Astaroth gives Loew a magic word that has to be written down and inserted into the figure's body to animate it.

Loew then brings the Golem to the Emperor's court during a feast, where he pleads for his people, conjuring up a vision of the Jews in the wilderness to show his nation's suffering. He warns his audience that if they value their lives they'd better watch carefully and not laugh. But they ignore him and the vision proves so powerful that it literally brings the house down, causing the near destruction of the Imperial palace. At this point the Emperor offers Loew a deal. If the Rabbi can save the palace, the Emperor will let the Jews off. So Loew calls on the Golem, who holds up the palace and the Jews are saved.

Meanwhile, back in the ghetto, Miriam, the Rabbi's seductive daughter, is entertaining the Emperor's messenger, Florian, in her boudoir. Her father returns and Florian is stuck, so he decides to hide until he can make his escape. Downstairs things are not going well with the Golem, who's started to rebel against his master. Loew looks up the small print in his magic book and realises that when the stars change to a certain constellation Astaroth takes over his creation - and this is just what's happened. Loew quickly removes the word of life from the monster and it turns back into clay. He is then called away to the celebrations for the Jewish salvation.

Florian sees his chance to escape, but just at that moment Famulus (Loew's assistant) turns up and realises that someone is in Miriam's room. This drives him crazy because he too has designs on her, so he brings the Golem back to life to get rid of his rival. Unfortunately the Golem is no longer in a listening mood, throws Florian off the roof of the house and then sets fire to the building. Chaos ensues and the Golem carries Miriam off. Eventually, after much confusion and panicking crowd scenes, Miriam is found unharmed. She makes up with Famulus (conveniently forgetting that her lover from the night before is still lying in pieces somewhere). Our attention now returns to the Golem who continues to roam. The next thing we see is the monster escaping the ghetto. He forces open the gate and comes across a group of children playing. He picks up a little girl, fascinated by her innocence and, as he holds her, she pulls the magic word from his body without a thought, turning him back to clay. The Golem is no more and everyone is saved.

Background: This telling of a traditional Jewish myth is a remake of Wegener and Galeen's 1914 film *Der Golem* which is now lost. The first version mixed contemporary events with the sixteenth century and had the Golem being rediscovered by workmen digging a well in an old synagogue. Like *Caligari*, the film's set is particularly impressive, designed by the famous architect Hans Poelzig, who planned the Großes Schauspielhaus in Berlin but who had fallen on hard times after the War. The ghetto is constructed as a claustrophobic labyrinth, full of strangely shaped buildings that stand at weird angles. But unlike *Caligari*, there is less of a theatrical feel to the film, mainly due to the use of much larger-scale sets. That's not to say, of course, that the film doesn't use devices from the world of theatre. As Lotte Eisner points out, Wegener was a product of the famous Max Reinhardt theatre troupe and translated lots of the lighting tricks he learnt there into film lighting, from the glistening stars we see as Loew predicts the future from the sky, to the image of blazing torches in the synagogue. Finally, you have to notice the obvious connection between Wegener's portrayal of the Golem as a thick-booted clay mammoth and Boris Karloff's portrayal of the monster in *Frankenstein* (1931), which must have been influenced by the earlier film.

Subtext: Although the film is considered to be a product of Expressionism in its film style, there's clearly a strong influence of earlier ages here. As Klaus Kreimer puts it, the film 'harkens back to an imaginary medieval era, to the relics of pre-industrial structures in the German (and European) psychic landscape.' Here we see the fantasy/horror film being used as a means of exploring the psychological underbelly of human nature, with the Golem's masters ultimately falling victim to the monster that has been created to fulfil their desires (a feature seen most clearly in the sequence where Famulus, driven by jealousy, brings the monster to life to kill his rival, only to see the monster destroy everything in its path). We also see the theme of cinema again: Loew's vision of the Jews in the wilderness plays like a film in the Emperor's court, turning the building into one big movie theatre. When the vision/film brings down destruction on the palace, Wegener, like Wiene before him, is clearly making a point about the power of the moving image to the audience of *Der Golem* itself.

So far we can see strong thematic and stylistic links with *Caligari*. Where it differs from this film is its anti-Semitism, which is even stronger here than it is in *The Student Of Prague*. The film portrays the Jews en mass as alien dabblers in the dark arts, complete with long wizard-like beards and pointed hats. In the extraordinary sequence where the Golem is brought to life amid a sea of fire and smoke, the link between Judaism and evil is made explicit when the Rabbi uses a glowing Star of David as a wand to call on the evil Astaroth. Although we see the Jews persecuted by the Christian majority, the spectator still has some sympathy with the Emperor who wishes to expel these foreign bodies from his society. The fact that we are not ultimately supposed to identify with the Jews is also highlighted by the narrow camera filters used in lots of shots of the ghetto, suggesting that the spectator is looking in at this Jewish world through a crack in the wall. The clichéd image of the Jew continues in the portrayal of the dark-haired beauty Miriam who, while not overtly luring her Christian lover to bed, certainly doesn't say no. Finally, the superiority of the Gentiles over the Jews is confirmed when the Golem is destroyed, not by Loew, but by a decidedly Aryan-looking child.

Verdict: Like *Caligari*, *Der Golem* is important for film history. In some ways it stands up better than Wiene's film because its plot seems more coherent. But, the anti-Semiticism of the film jars. 3/5

Das Wachsfigurenkabinett/Waxworks (1923)

Cast: Olga Belajeff (Eva-Maimune), William Dieterle (The Poet/The Baker/A Russian Prince), Emil Jannings (Harun al Raschid), Conrad Veidt (Ivan the Terrible), Werner Krauss (Jack the Ripper), John Gottowt (Waxworks Proprietor)

Crew: Directors Leo Birinsky and Paul Leni, Writer Henrik Galeen, Cinematography Helmar Lerski, Production Design Paul Leni

Story: A young man gets a job working for the proprietor of a waxworks at a fairground. His task is to write stories about the figures in the display to help bring in customers. As he sits down to write his first story, about Harun al Raschid, the Caliph of Baghdad, he notices the proprietor's daughter and is immediately attracted to her. In his story he imagines himself and the girl are married and living in Baghdad. He is a baker whose chimney disturbs the Caliph as he sits and plays a game of chess with the Vizier. The Caliph's not in the best of moods anyway because he is losing so he decides to behead the baker. He sends the Vizier down to do the job, but before the Vizier can carry out his orders he is distracted by the man's wife and so he does not complete his task. Clearly all is not well with the baker and his wife since she openly flirts with the Vizier. She is sick of being poor and tells her husband that he should be a man and do something about their situation. Egged on by the woman, he promises to steal the Caliph's magic wishing ring through which all their desires will be fulfilled and so off he goes to the palace.

Meanwhile the Caliph, having learnt from the Vizier of the beautiful baker's wife, decides to visit her at the same time as the baker has gone off to steal his ring. While he is trying it on with the woman the baker returns, having escaped from the palace (closely followed by palace guards), with his booty. Unfortunately it is still apparently attached to the Caliph's hand! How can this be since at this point the Caliph is hiding in the house? It turns out that the Caliph always leaves a wax figure in his bed when he sneaks out at night and it is this the baker has attacked. The wife thinks on her feet and finds a solution. She will pretend to use the wishing ring attached to the arm to bring the Caliph back to life. She fiddles with the ring and lo and behold, the Caliph appears from his hiding place. He is alive again, and the baker has been saved from being tried for murder. The Caliph, realising that he is not without blame in this situation (and with a bit of prodding from the baker's wife) pardons the man and gives him a job at his court.

In the second story we meet Ivan the Terrible Tsar of Russia who, for amusement, visits his torture chamber and looks at the victims he has had poisoned. He sees an hourglass, a favourite toy of his poisoner, who always writes the name of his victims on the glass. When all the sand runs out, the Tsar is informed, the victim dies. Ivan is then warned by an adviser not to trust the poisoner. He immediately acts upon this advice and has the man killed. But, before the man dies he manages to write the name of Ivan on his hourglass.

Meanwhile a wealthy man has come to bring Ivan to the wedding of his daughter. Fearing that it is a trap Ivan forces the man to swap places with him for the journey. Sure enough there is an assassination attempt on the way to the wedding and the bride's father is killed. Ivan refuses to let the guests mourn. He even decides to steal the bride for himself and have her husband tortured. That night, as the bride struggles with Ivan, the poisoner's hourglass is brought to the Tsar. He sees his name on it and believes himself to have been poisoned. He will only live until the last grain of sand has run through the hourglass. So, he frantically starts to turn the glass to stop the sand from running out, and continues turning it, we are told, for the rest of his days.

We return again to the waxworks, where the young man is still working. It is late now and the proprietor's daughter is asleep. The young man too is very tired and as he begins his final story, about Jack the Ripper, he falls asleep. He is plagued by a disturbing nightmare in which Jack chases the daughter through a ghostly fairground while the young man gives chase in an attempt to save her. Soon the man is woken up by the girl who realises that he is having a bad dream. We realise that she too has feelings for him and as she comforts him the couple are at last united.

Background: This, for the time, star-studded film was originally to have four stories - the final one being about Rinaldo Rinaldini - but this was never made. Although there are two directors credited, the main man behind the project was Paul Leni, with Birinsky only being allowed to deal with the actors. Clearly there is a big debt to *Caligari* owed here. Firstly, *Das Wachsfigurenkabinett* is similarly set in a fairground, the world of the carnival where the rules of normal, respectable society do not apply. Also the film employs a framing device, the story of the young poet being used as a tool to link the three horror stories. (Leni also appears to be borrowing from Fritz Lang's *Der Müde Tod/Destiny*.)

Like *Caligari* the Expressionist credentials of the film lay mainly in the *mise en scène*, although here chiaroscuro lighting is also central to the film's mood. In an article Leni wrote for the magazine *Kinematograph* in 1924, he claimed: 'I have tried to create sets so stylised that they evince no idea of reality. My fairground is sketched in with an utter renunciation of detail. All it seeks to engender is an indescribable fluidity of light, moving shapes, shadows, lines and curves. It is not extreme reality that the camera perceives, but the reality of the inner event, which is more profound, effective and moving than what we see through everyday eyes.' In the first episode Leni creates a wonderfully claustrophobic image of Baghdad, whose misshaped curved interiors also seem reminiscent of the Prague of *Der Golem*. The second story is much darker in tone. Here, the setting is complemented by Conrad Veidt's magnificent performance as Ivan the Terrible, whom we see driven to distraction as he obsessively turns the hourglass to stop his moment of death coming. Veidt's performance also greatly impressed the Russian director Sergei Eisenstein who later evoked Leni's film when he came to create the Russian despot on screen. But it is in the final story of Jack the Ripper that Leni's skill as an Expressionist film-maker really comes through. In this much shorter sequence physical reality dissolves into a nightmarish vision of abstract shapes and lights as the view of the fairground is subtly superimposed onto a series of internal shots, through which the ghostly figure of Jack floats. It doesn't really get more Expressionist than this, and indeed it is at this point that we begin to see the demise of Caligariesque abstraction.

Subtext: Once again we see Expressionism address the psychological state of the characters. Each story can be read as projections of the young man's fears and desires. On the one hand his construction of himself and the girl as a married couple in the first story is a reflection of his feelings of attraction towards her. However, their problematic marriage in the story also reflects his sense of anxiety and powerlessness towards the woman, who is in command of the relationship. In the final story, however, this power dynamic has changed. The man is now the woman's protector. It is as if he has worked through the sense of crisis in his masculinity which his feelings towards the girl has awoken and he can now approach her. That's one reading of the film, the other might be, of course, that Leni just wanted to figure out a way of linking up a string of one- or two-reel pictures into a feature.

Verdict: A classic piece of high Expressionism and very watchable, but perhaps there is a bit too much form and not enough content at times. It's certainly not in the same league as Fritz Lang, for example, to whom we now turn. 3/5

2. Fritz Lang (1890-1976)

Lang was born in Vienna in 1890 to a Catholic father and a Jewish mother. After school he studied painting briefly before setting off in 1910 to travel around Europe, ending up in Paris in 1913 where he took up his studies again. At the outbreak of the War he went back to Vienna and joined the army. In 1918 he was discharged with shell-shock and joined Pommer's company Decla. There he started out as a writer, but after the merger with Ufa he graduated to become the new company's star director. In 1922 he married the co-writer of many of his scripts, Thea von Harbou, but they were divorced in 1933 when Lang left Germany and she remained to work in the Nazi-controlled film industry. In exile, he initially went to Paris and then on to Hollywood, where he made some of the best *Films Noirs* of the 1940s and 1950s. In the 1950s his Hollywood work slowed down. This, Lang claimed, was a result of being blacklisted due to his previous collaboration with the Marxist dramatist Bertold Brecht on *Hangmen Also Die* (1946). There is, however, no actual evidence to back up his claims. In the late 1950s he returned to Germany to make his final three movies, the last being the third instalment in his Dr Mabuse trilogy, *Die Tausend Augen des Dr Mabuse/The Thousand Eyes Of Dr Mabuse* (1960).

Lang is probably the most important film-maker of the Expressionist era (although he claimed never to have anything to do with Expressionism). He had a huge influence on subsequent generations and is cited as a major inspiration for the likes of Luis Buñuel and Jean-Luc Godard. Lang's imagination and attention to detail, as well as his ability to put together a good crew, helped to accelerate massively the development of film as an art form. The following focuses on some of his most important silent films, but I'll be returning to Fritz Lang in the final chapter.

Der Müde Tod/Destiny (1921)

Cast: Max Adalbert (Notary/Chancellor), Grete Berger (Mother), Paul Biensfeldt (Ahi), Lewis Brody (Moor), Lil Dagover (Girl/Zobeide/Fiametta/Tiao Tsien), Bernhard Goetzke (Death/El Mot/Bogner), Walter Janssen (Lover/Franke/Giovanfrancesco/Liang), Georg John (Beggar), Rudolf Klein-Rogge (Dervish/Girolamo), Edgar Klitzsch (Apothecary), Karl Kuszar (Emperor), Lothar Müthel (Messenger), Paul Neumann (Executioner), Erich Pabst (Teacher), Lina Paulsen (Nurse), Max Pfeffer (Night Watchman), Hermann Picha (Tailor), Lydia Potechina (Landlady), Paul Rehkopf (Grave-digger), Ernst Rückert (Priest), Hans Sternberg (Mayor), Erika Unruh (Aisha), Marie Wismar (Old Woman), Eduard von Winterstein (Caliph)

Crew: Director Fritz Lang, Writers Fritz Lang and Thea von Harbou, Producer Erich Pommer, Cinematography Bruno Mondi, Erich Nitzschmann, Herrmann Saalfrank, Bruno Timm, Fritz Arno Wagner, Production Design Robert Herlth, Walter Röhrig, Hermann Warm, Decla

Story: A couple are on a trip to a quaint German village when a strange old man dressed completely in black gets into their carriage. This old man, we are told, came to the village years before and bought a plot of land next to the graveyard, around which he built a huge wall with no visible way in. The film then cuts to the couple arriving in the village and enjoying the hospitality of the local inn. The strange old man follows them and sits at their table, disturbing the girl, who feels him staring at her. The girl leaves the table for a moment and in the few minutes she is away her lover leaves with the old man.

In panic, the girl rushes out of the inn, desperately attempting to find her lover, until she arrives at the wall of the old man's garden. Here she sees a ghostly parade of spirits being led into the garden, her beloved amongst them. Suddenly she realises that the old man is Death and that this wall separates the realm of the living from the spirit world! She collapses at this revelation but luckily at that moment an apothecary, who is out collecting ingredients, comes along and takes her home with him. In the apothecary's house she happens to read one of the *Songs of Solomon*, in which she finds the line 'love is stronger than death.' Heartened by this she decides to take Death on. The clock strikes eleven; she picks up a bottle of poison, and as

34

she puts it to her lips she is transported back to the wall, which she can now pass through.

Once in Death's realm she pleads with him to release her loved one, but Death will not. However, he does take pity on her. Bringing her to a chamber full of candles, he explains that each candle is a human life. When one goes out it means that someone has died. He then points to three flickering flames and says that if she can stop even one of these candles from going out she can have her beloved back. We are then told the stories of the three flames and are transported from the caliphate of Baghdad, to Renaissance Venice and finally to ancient China. In each story, the girl has to save her lover from a vicious tyrant, and in each she fails. Each time Death is victorious.

Mercifully, Death decides to give her one more chance. If she can find someone willing to give up their life in exchange for her lover before the clock strikes midnight, he will still give the dead man back. The girl is returned to the apothecary. Strangely no time has passed. She awakes to find him knocking the poison out of her hand and so saving her life. She proceeds to reward this action by asking the old apothecary if he would like to give up his life; he has, after all, lived for many years. He refuses her offer claiming "Not one day, not one hour, not one breath" will he give up. The same response is given to her by a beggar she sees in the street.

Finally she goes to the hospital. Here she meets a group of old people in a sitting room who are weary of life; surely they will help her? But they too refuse and can't get away from the girl quick enough. As the old people rush out of the room a lamp is overturned and the hospital is set on fire. The patients are evacuated from the building but in the chaos a baby is left behind. Seeing her chance the girl rushes in. Death appears, ready to accept the baby, but just at the last moment, the girl is pricked by her conscience, and passes the baby out of the window into the arms of its frantic mother. At last she realises that the only person she can offer is herself and Death, kindly accepts her, uniting the girl at the stroke of midnight with her lover.

Background: This was the third collaboration between Lang and Thea von Harbou. It is Lang's first mature film and one which was clearly influenced by the fairy-tale/folklore world of Wegener's pre-War fantasy films. The use of the frame narrative to link different episodes furthermore echoes D.W. Griffith's *Intolerance* (1916), a film which links different stories with a common thread. *Der Müde Tod* has had a major influence on film-makers, from Luis Buñuel (who claimed that this film inspired him to become a director) to Ingmar Bergman and Terry Gilliam.

Part of the design team was Walter Röhrig, of *Caligari* fame, and you can see strong traces of Expressionism in the *mise en scène* and in the film's use of chiaroscuro lighting. However, in places, Lang deliberately seems to be trying to distance himself from pure Expressionism. Eisner notes, for example, that the story of the third candle, set in ancient China, could almost be seen as a parody of the sort of Expressionist set design found in earlier films: 'the overturned Baroque roofs built higgledy-piggledy together, the little bridges, the warped trees with their tortured curves and bends, are a good rendering of the bizarre contortions of Expressionism.' Yet, in this at times very humorous story of a good wizard who attempts to protect his daughter (the girl of the framing story) and her lover from the evil emperor, the *mise en scène* becomes nothing more than a comic background to the world of the clown-like magician.

Also worthy of mention is the sophistication of the camerawork and specifically the use of overlap-dissolve shots through which Lang creates the ghostly world of Death. For example, in the Hall of Candles, we see a baby appear and disappear in Death's hands above a flame as it flickers and goes out. Finally, you have to be impressed by the use of certain special effects, such as the illusion of a flying carpet and a miniature army conjured by the wizard in the third story.

Subtext: Fritz Lang claimed that the main theme of this film was the main theme of all his work: 'The fight of the individual against destiny is probably the basis of all my films, the struggle of a primarily good human being against higher and superior forces.' The girl finds it impossible to accept the edict of God, and wishes to cheat Death of her lover. But you can also turn this reading of the film on its head. If you do this, a strong thematic link can be found with the Expressionist artists of the pre-War period and their fear of the pace of modernity. Rather than being about the attempt to challenge the nature of destiny, the film could also be about the attempt to reaffirm the place of destiny in the world. Through the figure of Death, who pervades all the stories, the arbitrary events of different places and different times are imbued with a sense of logic, thereby giving order to the world. However, this order would seem to be on the wane, evoking once again the 'twilight of humanity' motif. Death is weary, desperate to have his authority challenged by this girl whom he allows to compete with him, and thus showing that he longs to be able to escape his duty as the messenger of God.

This theme is then linked explicitly to the problem of the increasing pace of modernity through the motif of the ticking clock, which, as Tom Gunning notes in his study of Lang, is central to the film. In the final segment of the narrative the girl is desperate to beat the forward march of time, which Gunning sees as a metaphor of unrelenting societal progress. However, this she ultimately fails to do. At the end of the film the girl is forced to give into time, sacrificing herself to destiny. Crucially, this in turn forces Death to accept his duty. As a result, order is maintained. The girl is finally rewarded by being allowed to escape time and to live for all eternity with her lover.

Verdict: This is a great movie, beautifully shot with impressive effects for the time and an excellent narrative. Without doubt 5/5

Dr Mabuse der Spieler/Dr Mabuse The Gambler (1922)

Cast: Alfred Abel (Count Told), Bernhard Goetzke (Public Prosecutor von Wenk), Aud Egede Nissen (Cara Carozza), Robert Forster-Larrinaga (Secretary Spoerri), Paul Richter (Eddie Hull), Rudolf Klein-Rogge (Dr Mabuse), Hans Adalbert Schlettow (Georg), Georg John (Pesch), Gertrud Welcker (Countess Told)

Crew: Director Fritz Lang, Writers Fritz Lang and Thea von Harbou, Novel Norbert Jacques, Producer Erich Pommer, Cinematography Carl Hoffmann, Production Design Otto Hunte and Stahl-Ubache, Ufa

Story: Dr Mabuse is a master criminal at the head of a huge underworld organisation, which he controls through meticulous attention to detail, his mastery of disguise and his ability to manipulate people's minds through hypnotism. In the course of the film we see him move from crime to crime, and from disguise to disguise, beginning with a train robbery, in which his stooges snatch some important trade documents. These Mabuse uses to manipulate the stock exchange, ruining hundreds of businessmen in the process. Next we see him using his mind-controlling powers to manipulate a wealthy young man, Eddie Hull, into gambling away all his money. Having nearly ruined the man, he decides to 'play' with him further by forcing the erotic dancer (and Mabuse's lover) Cara Carozza to have an affair with him, so that he can blackmail Hull at a later date.

At this point we meet the Public Prosecutor von Wenk (played by Bernhard Goetzke, who was Death in *Der Müde Tod*). Von Wenk has heard what has happened to Hull. He goes to the man to ask for help in tracking down an elusive villain, who he claims is behind a spate of crimes in the city. The film now slowly evolves into a battle of wills between von Wenk and Mabuse as the Public Prosecutor searches the nightclubs and casinos of the city for his prey. While on the hunt, von Wenk meets and falls for the world-weary Countess Told, who only goes to casinos to watch other people's misfortune. She offers to help the Public Prosecutor to find his man.

The duel between von Wenk and Mabuse develops into a battle for the two women, Carozza and Told. Each man is unable to destroy his opponent, so instead he captures the object of his opponent's desire. For most of the story Mabuse looks to have the upper hand. He kidnaps Told and although he makes two unsuccessful attempts on von Wenk's life, he eventually manages to hypnotise the man and to convince him to drive his car off a cliff. However, just at the moment when von Wenk is about to die, he is pulled from the car by the police. He remembers who hypnotised him and so at last knows who Mabuse is.

Finally von Wenk and the police track down Mabuse's lair. They save the Countess and capture his gang, but Mabuse escapes down an underground passage to a cellar where his counterfeiting operation takes place. Mabuse's days are now numbered. Having pulled the trap door of the cellar behind him, he realises he is locked in. The fact that he is trapped begins to drive him insane. We see him plagued by hallucinatory visions of all his victims; even the counterfeiting press comes to life and seems to attack him. With his underworld empire now in ruins, he buries himself in a pile of counterfeit money in an attempt to escape the hallucinations, at which point the police finally arrive and Mabuse is led away.

Background: The film is in two parts. Part One is subtitled 'A portrait of our time' and Part Two 'Inferno characters of the time' and the running time for both films is almost five hours. I mention this because there are shorter versions of the film available in which both parts are edited together. Be careful with these because they leave out many of the pivotal scenes. In *Dr Mabuse* we see Lang and (his now wife) von Harbou return to the genre of the detective story Lang first took up in *Die Spinnen* (the film that stopped him directing *Caligari*). Both films were greatly influenced by the exotic pulp detective series found in the daily newspapers at the time. However, in *Dr Mabuse*, there is a far greater level of complexity than in *Die Spinnen*. On the one hand the duel between Mabuse and von Wenk recalls the classic world of Conan Doyle and the battle between Sherlock Holmes and his arch-rival Moriarty. On the other it prefigures the struggle between James Bond and his super villains. Indeed the obsession with gadgetry you find in the Bond films, which are full of fast cars fitted with special weapons and revolving number plates, would seem to be lifted directly from *Dr Mabuse*. And it's not only the content of the film that prefigures later developments. The marketing strategy used to sell *Dr Mabuse* would also point the way forward for the movie industry through its use of a multimedia advertising campaign. As Elsaesser notes, the film's premiere was timed to coincide with a serialisation of the novel with one being used to promote the other.

We also see Lang here continue to ironise Expressionist style, which we see him invoke in the underworld clubs where von Wenk and Mabuse clash. Rather than Expressionist *mise en scène* being used to show the psychological depth of the film's characters as it is in *Caligari*, here it's used to highlight the superficial decadence of the world we are watching. Expressionism, the dominant style of the times, becomes a metaphor for the state of society. "It's just a game," Mabuse says at one point when asked what he thinks of the Expressionist painting he is looking at. Mabuse then suggests that Expressionism is the perfect style for the times because "today everything is just a game." Expressionism, like Weimar Germany, is empty of meaning. It is all form and no content.

Subtext: It's difficult to know where to start with this one, the film works on so many different levels. We see some of the preoccupations that we've already talked about in other films. For example, we are again asked to question the relationship between the audience and film. After all, the way Mabuse controls his victims is by making them stare into his eyes, something which he then invites the cinema audience to do by staring directly into the camera.

The relationship of the film to technology and modern life generally is, moreover, far more pronounced in this film than any of the others we have looked at so far. As the subtitle of Part One suggests, it is 'A portrait of our time.' While *Der Müde Tod* might have had some oblique references to the present, *Dr Mabuse* is set in the centre of the chaos of early Weimar society. Eisner claims that the opening of the film was to be a montage of violent scenes from the Communist revolution of 1919, as well as the right-wing attempted coup that followed it. This sequence was then linked to the opening of the film we now have with two intertitles, the first being 'Who is behind it all?' and the second a single word: 'Mabuse.'

Mabuse is the force behind the chaos of modern society. In the existing film this is suggested most clearly in the stock exchange sequence. At the end of a day's trading that has seen the ruin of so many men's lives, the stock market is left empty, its floor covered by scraps of paper from discarded order forms. The face of the mysterious businessman who is the only one to have made any money that day slowly appears over the scene. This face then fades out and is replaced by the sinister image of Dr Mabuse without his disguise. In 1921, when the movie was being shot, the country's financial system was in the meltdown that, two years later, would lead to hyperinflation. Thus by superimposing the image of Mabuse over the stock exchange Lang links the actual experience of the audience with the fiction of the film, suggesting in the mind of the spectator that his fictional character is truly the mastermind of the present societal crisis.

To a degree, Mabuse is like Death in the earlier film. He gives meaning to the apparently arbitrary nature of modern life. Mabuse is a force of evil, but even an evil organising force is better than meaningless chaos. Also, once you know it's Mabuse who's behind it all you can then try and catch him. However, if you start to probe deeper, Mabuse as the image of destiny is far more problematic than that of Death. Firstly, he can't be pinned down. When von Wenk first sets out to find him he has no idea what Mabuse is; he just knows that he ought to exist. Mabuse's power lies in his ability to mutate, to become whatever is needed, like an ever-changing virus. Also, the film deliberately sets up parallels between von Wenk and Mabuse, repeatedly intercutting between the two men. As a result we feel less than comfortable that all is well when Mabuse is carried off at the end of the film.

Our sense of discomfort at the end of the film might also be related to the theme of society as a 'game' already mentioned. Central to the film is the theme of playing. The German title 'der Spieler' means both gambler and player. Perhaps, rather than being the force behind present evil, Mabuse is simply a product of a society in which superficiality and game-playing, such as we have seen in the constant casino sequences, are the only purposes left. Here Lang seems again to be ahead of the times, perhaps inventing the notion of life and art as a 'postmodern' joke at a time when 'modernism' was only just getting going. Rather than giving society meaning (however uncomfortable that meaning might be), perhaps Mabuse just flags up the meaninglessness of society.

Verdict: This is one of Lang's best, a fast-paced, highly complex analysis of Weimar life. If you only watch one silent film by Lang, make it this one. 5/5

Die Nibelungen/The Nibelungen (1924)

Cast: Paul Richter (Siegfried), Margarete Schön (Kriemhild), Hanna Ralph (Brunhild), Gertrud Arnold (Queen Ute), Theodor Loos (King Gunther), Hans Carl Mueller (Gernot), Erwin Siswanger (Giselher), Bernhard Goetzke (Volker von Alzey), Georg John (Mime, the Smith/Alberich, der Nibelung), Hans Adalbert Schlettow (Hagen Tronje), Hardy von Francois (Dankwart), Georg Jurowski (The Priest), Rudolf Klein-Rogge (Etzel), Georg John (Slaodel), Hubert Heinrich (Werbel, The Bard), Rudolf Rittner (Rüdiger von Bechlarn), Aenne Roettgen (Dietlind), Fritz Alberti (Dietrich von Bern), Georg August Koch (Hildebrand)

Crew: Director Fritz Lang, Writers Fritz Lang and Thea von Harbou, Producer Erich Pommer, Cinematography Carl Hoffmann, Günther Rittau, Walter Ruttmann, Production Design Otto Hunte and Karl Vollbrecht, Ufa

Story: Like *Dr Mabuse*, *Die Nibelungen* was made in two parts, *Siegfried* and *Kriemhilds Rache/Kriemhild's Revenge*, but here Lang leaves present-day society and travels back to the world of Germanic mythology. In part one we meet the film's eponymous hero as he learns of the beautiful Kriemhild, who he declares he will marry. He then sets off on an epic journey to her home in the court of Burgundy. On the way he is forced to fight the dragon Fafnir and by bathing in its blood makes himself all but invincible. The only fly in the ointment is that as he bathed a Linden leaf fell on his back, stopping the dragon's blood from completely covering him. Consequently he remains vulnerable in one spot. Having survived the dragon, he is then attacked by Alberich, the Keeper of the treasure of the Nibelungen. But Alberich is no match for Siegfried. Siegfried defeats him and gains both the immense wealth of the Nibelungen, and crucially for the rest of the film, Alberich's net of invisibility.

At last he arrives at Kriemhild's home. Before he can marry the girl he must help her brother King Gunther win his bride, the untameable Brunhild Queen of Iceland. Siegfried tricks the woman into accepting Gunther by making himself invisible and helping the King to beat her in a series of athletic games. With Brunhild conquered, they all return to Burgundy and Siegfried marries Kriemhild. Brunhild soon learns the truth about her husband, that it was not Gunther who conquered her and sets about plotting Siegfried's destruction. She manages to get Gunther's loyal champion, Hagen, to trick Kriemhild into revealing the chink in Siegfried's invulnerability. Then, on a hunting trip Hagen plunges his spear into the spot on Siegfried's back where the leaf had settled and our hero dies. At his funeral Kriemhild swears revenge and so the scene is set for the second film, *Kriemhilds Rache*.

This film opens with Kriemhild receiving a proposal of marriage from Etzel, King of the Huns. Kriemhild accepts, provided that Etzel will help her in her hunt for justice for the murder of Siegfried. This Etzel promises to do. Kriemhild bears her new husband a son and asks him if he will invite her brother to visit them, hoping that this will give Etzel the opportunity to carry out his oath of revenge. The proud King refuses to kill a man who is a guest at his house, so Kriemhild looks for other methods. After some persuasion she manages to incite the Hun masses to attack her brother and his entourage. A huge battle ensues, in which Hagen, the murderer of Siegfried, also kills Etzel's son. As the battle goes on, the Huns are ejected from the banqueting hall, where the Burgundians remain trapped. Now the King too wants revenge, declaring, with his wife that if they give up the murderer the rest can go free. The proud Burgundians refuse to betray one of their comrades and there ensues a terrible mass slaughter when Kriemhild orders the banqueting hall to be set alight.

In the resulting fire nearly all her brother's supporters are destroyed; only her brother and the murderer Hagen remain. These two leave the burning building, only to be killed by Kriemhild. Revenge has been achieved, but due to her efforts Kriemhild is left exhausted and she too expires. In the final scene, we see her taken off for burial by Etzel, the man who loved her, but whom she only ever used as a tool in her self-destructive drive to avenge her first husband.

Background: We now enter the period of those epic films for which Lang is to a large extent remembered today. The *Nibelungen* films, along with his next project, *Metropolis*, were directly affected by Pommer and Lang's trip to the States, a trip which taught them to think big. In *Siegfried* and *Kriemhilds Rache* Lang creates four separate mythical worlds, all of huge proportions, which range from the geometric architecture of the court of the Burgundians to the teaming, organic primitivism of the realm of King Etzel. As we've already seen in Lang's other films, special effects play an important role. What most people pick out here is the sequence in which Siegfried fights the huge fire-breathing dragon Fafnir. Lang had a massive model of the monster built, which was operated by sixteen people, and managed to produce a pretty realistic beast for the time and one which still looks impressive today. The camerawork in the film was groundbreaking, as it generally is in Lang's work, with Hoffmann and Rittau always managing to keep up with the director's vivid imagination. And Lang wasn't unaware of their importance for his films. As Eisner tells us in her programme notes to *Die Nibelungen*, Lang claims that he was always impressed by the fact that the cameramen would sometimes experiment for whole nights to work out a specific trick. In *Die Nibelungen*, the superimposing of one image on another is taken to a new level of sophistication, most famously in the sequence where the dwarves that hold up the treasure of the Nibelungen are slowly turned into stone from their feet upwards. Also, lighting is used to great effect. Have a look, for example, at the magnificent sequence where Brunhild waits for the Burgundians and we see the aurora borealis flickering across the screen. This was an innovative effect at the time, which Rittau achieved by shining spotlights onto a moving mirror.

Subtext: In choosing the myth of the Nibelungen for this project Lang and Harbou wanted to make a truly German epic, which could then be exported around the world. Initially it was this nationalistic element that was praised by critics. As Eisner notes, *Siegfried* was seen as 'by birth and character "the most German of men."' Similarly the bravery of King Gunther's supporters, who refuse to give up Hagen to Kriemhild was taken as an image of the fidelity of the German people. Kracauer adopts this reading in his study of Weimar film. However, rather than praising the ostensibly nationalistic elements in the film, he claims that they foreshadow some of the more dodgy developments of the German national character under the Nazis, suggesting that images like the dwarves turning into stone statues prefigure the images found in Leni Riefenstahl's Nazi propaganda films such as *Triumph of the Will* (1935). In Riefenstahl's film for example, all individuality is lost as humans are reduced to massive geometrical spectacles that march before their Führer.

There are lots of images (intentional or not) in Lang's film that were later attractive to the Nazis. Gunning points out, for example, the fact that Siegfried was stabbed in the back, recalling the common view at the time that Germany had only lost the First World War because it had been 'stabbed in the back' by its leaders. But in the 1960s Lang questioned such a one-sided reading of the film. He points out, for example, some of Siegfried's weaknesses, claiming that it's easy to a great hero if you've got an invisibility cloak, and highlighting the fact that his final destruction comes in part from his bragging to his wife that he won Brunhild for the king (a piece of information Kriemhild then lets slip).

Verdict: Two more great films which see Lang continue to develop as a film-maker. 5/5

Metropolis (1926)

Cast: Alfred Abel (Jon Fredersen), Gustav Fröhlich (Freder Fredersen), Brigitte Helm (Maria/The Robot), Rudolf Klein-Rogge (C.A. Rotwang), Fritz Rasp (Slim), Theodor Loos (Josaphat), Heinrich George (Grot)

Crew: Director Fritz Lang, Writers Fritz Lang and Thea von Harbou, Producer Erich Pommer, Cinematography Karl Freund, Günther Rittau, Production Design Otto Hunte, Erich Kettelhut, Karl Vollbrecht, Visual Effects Eugen Schüfftan, Ufa

Story: We are at the beginning of the twenty-first century in a vast city complex, full of towering buildings and sky-bound walkways. Welcome to Metropolis. In the city's roof gardens the sons and daughters of the city's rulers indulge in a life of endless parties, whilst deep in its bowels the working masses are treated like drones, toiling endlessly to maintain the machines that keep Metropolis working. One day a beautiful young woman,

Maria (played by the huge Ufa star Brigitte Helm), brings a group of children from the workers' level up to one of the roof gardens to prick the conscience of the ruling class. She meets Freder Fredersen, who immediately becomes infatuated with her and follows her back down to the workers' world. Here Freder sees how the masses live, learning how human lives are sacrificed to the needs of the machines in the city.

Driven by a wish to change things, he goes to his father, the Lord of Metropolis, Jon Fredersen. But the father ignores his son's pleas, so Freder decides to go back down to the workers' level. Meanwhile his father learns that there is a plot hatching amongst the workers and that they have been meeting in secret. He goes to the house of a mad inventor, Rotwang, and asks for his help in dealing with the workers. While there he is shown Rotwang's new invention, a robot. If Jon can populate the city with these he'll no longer need his inefficient human workers. The two men descend to the workers' level and secretly spy on the meeting, to which Freder has also gone. The meeting is led by the beautiful woman from the garden. Constructed as a very thinly disguised image of the Virgin Mary, Maria preaches forbearance. The workers must be patient, for one day their saviour will come, a mediator, or as she puts it, a "Heart" to stand between the "Head" (the Lord of the city) and the "Hand" (the workers). She looks at Freder - is he their saviour? As the meeting ends Freder is united with the beautiful woman.

Jon decides that Maria must go. They kidnap her and take her back to Rotwang's laboratory where they produce a robotic version of the woman. This robot Maria is the complete opposite of the real thing. She is a wild-eyed, destructive monster who can whip her audience into a frenzy. The bad Maria takes the next meeting telling those who attend that they should not endure their plight, that they should revolt and destroy the machines that constrain them. Realising that this is not the real Maria, Freder goes off in search of his love. Meanwhile, the city descends into chaos as the workers storm the machines that oppress them.

But, little do the workers know that in destroying the machines they are also destroying their homes and putting the lives of their children at risk, since one of the machines' functions is to keep the water out of the bowels of the city where they live. Now that the machines are gone, the water starts to flood in. Luckily the good Maria has escaped from Rotwang's house. She manages to warn the workers in time and, having joined up with Freder again, the couple lead the children to safety. Elsewhere some of the workers are looking for Maria, blaming her for the city's near destruction. They find the robot and burn it at the stake. Freder is devastated, thinking that this is the real Maria, and goes to try and save her. In the process, he gets into a fight with Rotwang, causing the evil inventor to tumble to his death. Eventually calm returns and in the final sequence we see the workers marching up the stairs of a church towards Jon. Under the supervision of Freder, one of the workers joins hands with Jon. Maria's prophecy has been fulfilled. The Hand and the Head have been linked by the Heart. Metropolis' future is secure and the workers' plight will now improve.

Background: Metropolis is probably Fritz Lang's most famous film and its production was a huge undertaking. Lang used 37,633 performers and spent 5.3 million Marks, making it the most expensive German film of its age. The production costs of the film nearly bankrupted Ufa, with the company only surviving through the intervention of Paramount. It was originally 17 reels long, but was cut down to 10 for its American release, most of the cuts coming from a sub-plot concerning a love triangle between Jon, Rotwang and Freder's mother Hel (in most versions of the film she is mentioned without any explanation as to who she is).

It is also considered by many to be the first modern science fiction movie (although it was made some 24 years after Georges Méliès' 1902 film *A Trip To The Moon*), and certainly the vision of the city of Metropolis has become a standard way to represent 'the future.' Lang's *mise en scène* is continually evoked in contemporary Sci-fi, most famously in Ridley Scott's *Blade Runner* (1982). Lang originally got the idea for his image of Metropolis when he first saw the New York skyline from the boat on his trip to the States in 1924. In a particularly touching tribute to Lang, Giuseppe Tornatore reversed this influence in *The Legend Of 1900* (1998) by turning the New York skyline itself into an image of Metropolis, which the film's hero, like Lang, views from his ship. As with Lang's other films, the use of technology has to be mentioned. In *Metropolis* we see the invention of what has become known as the Schüfftan Process. Named after the film's visual effects man Eugen Schüfftan, the Schüfftan Process was a highly innovative technique in which mirrors and miniature sets were used to create the illusion of size. This is used particularly effectively in many of the film's city-scape shots.

Subtext: Metropolis is a nightmarish vision of the future, in which the processes of modernity, well underway by the 1920s, have been allowed to reach their natural conclusion unchecked. Machines dominate the world and all human individuality has been lost. Attitudes towards the film have largely been coloured by an anecdote told by Lang about it. *Metropolis* was, apparently, Hitler's favourite film. When the Nazis came to power Goebbels was instructed to ask Lang (who was half Jewish) to become their official film-maker. Lang claimed that he immediately excused himself and left the country the same day. The biographer Patrick McGilligan points out, though, that Lang only began to tell this story in the 1940s, and suggests that he used it to help promote his anti-Nazi war films such as *Hangmen Also Die*.

Whether or not the film was Hitler's favourite, it does, on one level at least, have a strong right-wing message. This is no film preaching proletarian revolution. Capitalism is in essence good. It just needs a strong and benevolent leader, the Heart, who can look after the needs of the masses and temper the more extreme impulses of the industrialists (enter Adolf Hitler). However, the effectiveness of this right-wing message is undermined somewhat by the abrupt and rather crass ending, in which the Hand and Head of the city are united, only moments after the workers have been knocking seven bells out of the industrialists' machines. Is this just a piece of bad writing? Probably. Lang claimed he never really liked the film's final sequence. But in some ways the crass ending might also save the film, preventing the audience from buying into von Harbou's simplistic message, thereby hinting at the fact that the relationship between the workers and their bosses in the real world is generally a bit more complicated than the film suggests.

Verdict: This is clearly an important film and probably Lang's most famous, but I don't find it as compelling as some of the others, mainly due to the massive cuts that are in the version we now have, which make some of the story illogical. 4/5

3. Friedrich Wilhelm Murnau (1888-1931)

F.W. Murnau was born F.W. Plumpe in Bielfeld in 1888. In 1907 he began to study Art History and Philosophy in Berlin. However he soon realised that his first love was the theatre and in 1911 he joined Max Reinhardt's theatre school. In 1913 he met some of the Expressionists, such as Paul Zech and Else Lasker-Schüler, and became very interested in their work, in particular the fraught image of the world they presented. On the outbreak of World War One he joined the air force and spent most of his time in Switzerland, where he also started to make films (none of which have survived). After the War Murnau returned to Berlin to direct *Der Knabe in Blau/The Blue Boy* (1919). However, he had to wait another year for his first hit, *Der Gang in die Nacht/Journey Into The Night* (1920). The international success of *Der letzte Mann/The Last Laugh* (1925) brought him to the attention of Hollywood. He signed a deal with Fox and whilst staying with the writer with whom he worked on *Der letzte Mann,* Carl Mayer (of *Caligari* fame), he made his first English-language masterpiece, *Sunrise* (1927). This was followed by *Four Devils* (1928) and *City Girl* (1930). Murnau didn't have great commercial success with Fox and eventually they parted company, leaving him to make his final film independently: *Tabu* (1931), which was shot entirely on location in the South Seas. Tragically, however, Murnau never saw the film's premiere as he was killed in a car crash in Santa Monica in 1931.

Nosferatu: eine Symphonie des Grauens/
Nosferatu: A Symphony Of Terror (1921)

Cast: Max Schreck (Count Orlok/Nosferatu), Alexander Granach (Broker Knock), Gustav von Wangenheim (Thomas Hutter), Greta Schröder (Ellen Hutter), Georg H. Schnell (Westrenka), Ruth Landshoff (Lucy Westrenka), John Gottowt (Professor Bulwer), Gustav Botz (Dr Sievers), Max Nemetz (Captain), Wolfgang Heinz (First mate)

Crew: Director F.W. Murnau, Writer Henrik Galeen, Novel *Dracula* by Bram Stoker (uncredited), Producer Enrico Dieckmann and Albin Grau, Cinematography Günther Krampf and Fritz Arno Wagner, Production Design Albin Grau, Jofa-Atelier Berlin-Johannisthal and Prana-Film

Story: It is 1838 and the estate agent Thomas Hutter has been asked to go to Transylvania to sell a house to Count Orlok. Saying farewell to his new wife he eagerly travels to the Count's remote castle. Here he meets the frightening, hardly human-looking, Orlok. They talk deep into the night and the next morning Thomas wakes up to find himself with two bite marks on his neck. Slowly Thomas realises that his host is a vampire, the legendary Nosferatu. But, it is too late. Trapped in the castle, the man cannot escape as Nosferatu comes to his room at night to suck his blood.

Meanwhile in Bremen, Thomas' wife, Ellen, is having a disturbed dream. She knows that something is wrong with her husband and calls out to him in her sleep. The Count senses Ellen's psychic connection to Thomas and turns away from his victim, deciding instead to travel to Bremen to take this woman. He buries himself in a stack of coffins filled with soil (Vampires must always sleep in the same ground in which they were buried) and sets off for Germany by boat. As he travels he brings plague and pestilence to the whole of the ship's crew, who all die, and to every port he calls at. Finally he arrives in Bremen, which then also becomes engulfed by disease.

Back in Transylvania Thomas has escaped the castle and is hurrying back to Ellen to warn her of Nosferatu's intentions. Once reunited, Ellen fears that Nosferatu will return to continue feeding on her husband to turn him into a vampire, so she tries to find a way of destroying the monster. She discovers the 'Book of Vampires,' in which she learns that if a woman pure of heart sacrifices herself freely to the vampire and manages to keep him in their room until the cock crows then his power is lost. Ellen decides that she will give herself up to save her husband. She entices the Count to her room, who feeds off her until dawn, at which point he simply vanishes in a puff of smoke. For a brief moment Ellen raises her head as her husband comes into her room. Tragically there is nothing he can do. Both he and the town are saved but she has lost all her blood and so dies in Thomas' arms.

Background: This is the first important vampire film to be made and it set the standard by which others are still judged today. The movie was based loosely on Bram Stoker's *Dracula* (1897). Unfortunately, nobody asked permission to use the novel and Murnau was sued by the novelist's widow, eventually being ordered to destroy all the prints of the film. Luckily, not all of them were lost. Unlike *Caligari* and *Wachsfigurenkabinett*, the Expressionist credentials of this film are not to be found in the set design, but in the way the film is shot. The jarring abstraction of the painted world of Holstenwall is rendered here by low-angle camera shots, lighting and montage sequences.

The vast majority of this film was shot on location in Central Europe, and Murnau makes great use of the landscape, with Fritz Arno Wagner's stunning images of the cloud-covered sky conveying beautifully the eeriness of Transylvania. The external shots came about by the need to make a virtue out of necessity. This was an independent production and Murnau didn't have the resources necessary to build the massive internal studio sets found in Lang's work.

A good deal of the film's power comes from the performance of Max Schreck as the huge, rat-like vampire. Myths abound about Schreck, who apparently never appeared on the set without his make-up. His surname means 'fright' in German, and is clearly a stage name, but it is claimed that at least at the time nobody knew his true identity. This has led to many rumours about him, from stories of him being a criminal on the run, to those who believe that he was a vampire, a rumour which became the basis for Elias Merhige's 2000 film *Shadow Of The Vampire*.

Subtext: In his adaptation of Bram Stoker's novel, Galeen was particularly concerned to bring out the moral aspects of the story, thus constructing the narrative primarily as a fight between good and evil. This he does by placing the relationship of Thomas and Ellen and their psychic connection centre stage. However, beneath this story we can perhaps once again see the anti-Semitic tendencies that we have met elsewhere in Weimar film. As

Anton Kaes points out, in the early part of the twentieth century there was an influx of Jews into Germany from Eastern and Central Europe. In the figure of Nosferatu, 'the foreign intruder from distant Transylvania, a region of Rumania, from where a lot of Eastern Jews came' we can see many of the visual associations of later more overtly anti-Semitic images, such as Fritz Hippler's 1940 Nazi propaganda film *Der Ewige Jude/The Eternal Jew* in which, for example, you also find a connection between Jews and rats.

That said, the film can't be reduced to this one reading. Elsaesser, for instance, points out the sophisticated psychological dimension of the film, which explores that old favourite of Weimar Expressionism, the nature of desire. In Elsaesser's reading, the vampire is Thomas' double. Thomas can't wait to run away from his wife at the beginning of the film to go to Transylvania, Nosferatu, on the other hand, longs to meet her. He is full of desire for the woman and ultimately it is his relationship to Ellen which is central to the film, not that of Thomas. Again, just as we have seen in *Caligari*, the passion of desire has a flip side. Sexual yearning is repaid by death and destruction.

Verdict: Murnau has often been called a poetic film-maker and Nosferatu is the most famous example of this. 5/5

Der letzte Mann/The Last Laugh (1924)

Cast: Emil Jannings (Doorman), Maly Delschaft (His Niece), Max Hiller (Her Bridegroom), Emilie Kurz (Bridegroom's Aunt), Hans Unterkircher (Hotel Manager), Olaf Storm (Young Guest), Hermann Vallentin (Guest with Potbelly), Georg John (Night Watchman), Emmy Wyda (Thin Neighbour)

Crew: Director F.W. Murnau, Writer Carl Mayer, Producer Erich Pommer, Cinematography Robert Baberske and Karl Freund, Production Design Robert Herlth and Walter Röhrig, Ufa

Story: The doorman of the Atlantis hotel is proud of his job and even prouder of his gold-braided uniform. In it he commands the respect not only of people at work, but also of his neighbours who bow and scrape before him as he walks to and from the hotel. But unfortunately the man is getting on in years and is no longer able to carry the heavy cases of the guests. So he is forced to hand back his uniform and is, instead, given a job as the hotel's lavatory attendant.

He is a broken man. But that night as he leaves the hotel he comes up with a plan to steal back the uniform so that he can pretend to his family, his neighbours and ultimately himself that he is still the doorman. The next day he walks to work in a daze, trying to suppress what happened the day before. When he arrives at the hotel this proves impossible. He sees some-one else in his position and is forced to face the fact that he has lost his prized job. He removes the uniform and takes up his duties giving towels to the great and the good in his lavatory. During the day, one of his neighbours comes to work to bring him his lunch. Realising that he has been replaced she rushes home to tell his family and the rest of the neighbourhood. The family feels humiliated whilst the neighbours are gripped by *Schadenfreude* for the man they have always looked up to in the past. He is turned out of his home and in a state of complete despair he returns to the hotel, where he gets the night watchman to put his uniform back in its cupboard. At last he has accepted his fate. We then see the man descend into the lavatory, where he finally slumps against the wall, destroyed by the hotel's treatment of him. As he falls asleep he is covered up by the night watchman.

The film then takes a farcical turn. The only intertitle of the film tells us that in reality the man would spend the rest of his days working in the lava-tory, but the writer has taken pity on him and decided to give him a different ending. We then move to the epilogue where we discover that the man has inherited a large fortune from a millionaire who died in his toilet. Curiously the rich man's will had a clause in it, stating that his fortune was to go to the person in whose arms he died - this was our hero. In the film's final sequence we see the man indulging himself and his friend the night watch-man in the hotel's restaurant. He has been saved from humiliation and pre-sumably lives happily ever after.

Background: This is the film which established Murnau's name as an important director and, although it is often termed Expressionist, really it belongs to the more realist films which began to be made from the middle of the 1920s onward - specifically to the genre of the *Kammerfilm*, or 'Cham-ber film.' These films tended to focus on a moment of crisis in the lives of a small group of characters, generally from the lower-middle class. That said, there is still a strong Expressionistic hangover here (after all, a lot of the crew, including the writer Carl Mayer had worked on *Caligari*). What makes this film stand out is the cinematography, and particularly Karl Freund's use of what was termed the entfesselte Kamera, or 'unchained camera,' a development which completely changed the nature of film-making. Up until that point the camera had generally been static. Narrative was developed purely through the performance of the actors and the director's editing. Now the camera itself became an actor in the film. For example, in the famous opening sequence the camera becomes a guest in the hotel as it travels down the lift and up to the revolving doors of the lobby, where we meet the doorman. Freund achieved this effect by putting the camera on a bicycle. Later in the film he strapped the camera to himself and staggered around a room to create the effect of the doorman being drunk. Thus, the camera allows the spectator to enter the subjective reality of the characters. This then takes us back to Expressionism and the impulse to express the inner world of the characters. As David A. Cooke has pointed out, 'Quite frequently, in addition to assuming the position of the doorman's physical eye, the camera assumes the position of his mind's eye as well.' In one particularly powerful sequence, for example, Murnau inserts a piece of montage in which we see in close-up an abstract collage of the distorted laughing face of one of the neighbours, symbolically suggesting the inner turmoil the man is going through. We also see aspects of Expressionism in the use of high and low angle shots which similarly highlight the psychological state of the man. At the beginning, for example, he is filmed from below, a perspective which emphasises his height in relationship to the people he meets. Then, when he loses his job the camera is above him, thus emphasising the sense that he has been crushed.

The only disappointment with this film is the 'happy ending,' which apparently wasn't Mayer's or Murnau's idea. By now working for Ufa, Murnau was forced to comply with Pommer's wishes, who insisted upon this ending, because Americans didn't like sad films. To Pommer's credit the film was a huge hit but Mayer's feeling towards the ending perhaps explains why the only intertitle in the film is inserted just before the epilogue, to draw the audience's attention to the farcical nature of the man becoming a millionaire.

Subtext: Eisner claims that this film could only have been made in Germany: 'This is pre-eminently a German tragedy, and can only be understood in a country where uniform is King.' As other critics have also noted, the film seems to foreshadow the obsession with uniform that would come with the pageantry of National Socialism. All status is dependant on the man's clothing. However, on another level the film is about the more universal issue of growing old and of being out of step with the times. The old man is a product of the Wilhelmian age (as can be seen in Jannings' dress and bushy facial hair) whereas the new doorman is a product of Weimar. So we see again the preoccupation with the process of modernity, of society changing and the problems of keeping up with this change. These are issues which we already saw in Lang's films, but here, due to the increased subjectivity the unchained camera brings to the film, they are dealt with on a far more intimate level than in, say, *Dr Mabuse*.

Verdict: As in *Nosferatu* it's the cinematography that is most impressive in this film, but here we really do see genius at work. 5/5

Tartüff/Tartuffe (1925)

Cast: Lil Dagover (Elmire, Orgon's Wife), Lucie Höflich (Dorine), Emil Jannings (Tartüff), Werner Krauss (Orgon), André Mattoni (Grandson), Hermann Picha (Old Councillor), Rosa Valetti (Housekeeper)

Crew: Director F.W. Murnau, Writers Carl Mayer, Molière, Producer Erich Pommer, Cinematography Karl Freund, Production Design Robert Herlth and Walter Röhrig, Ufa

Story: A young man is desperate to save his grandfather, an old councillor, from the clutches of his money-grubbing housekeeper. She is attempting to swindle the old man out of his fortune by getting him to make over his will to her, whilst at the same time gradually poisoning him. Although the housekeeper attempts to keep the young man out of the house, he manages to find a way in. He tries to speak to his grandfather but the old councillor is completely under the sway of the housekeeper and so the young man is evicted from the house. But the grandson is not to be put off. He is an actor and so hatches a cunning plan to show up the woman.

He disguises himself as the proprietor of a travelling cinema. He returns to the house and offers to give the housekeeper and the old man a show. "What film do you have?," the housekeeper asks. "Tartüff," he replies, a story about priests and religion. This sounds very suitable and so she allows him in. We are then given a film within a film of Molière's comedy *Tartuffe*, the story of a rich count who falls under the spell of a swindler. This swindler pretends to be a holy man and uses his religious guise to trick his victims into giving them all his money. Unable to convince her husband that this Tartuffe is a conman, his wife resorts to the desperate tactics of allowing herself to be seduced by him while her housekeeper makes sure that her husband is there to see it. The man now sees Tartuffe for what he is, and he expels the swindler from his house.

The film now returns to the present. The grandson attempts to make a link between the film and the grandfather's predicament, but to no avail, so he reveals his true identity and accuses the woman outright of abusing her charge. The woman is livid, but during her angry outburst she reveals her true colours and, as she tries to make amends with the grandfather, the grandson finds the bottle of poison she has been giving the old man. At last he sees her for what she really is and she is thrown out of the house to the taunts of a gang of children playing outside.

Background: Eager to capitalise on the success of *Der letzte Mann*, Pommer kept the same team together for Murnau's next project, a big-budget production of Molière's play. Carl Mayer then added the framing device of the story of the grandson and the travelling cinema. Here we see Murnau continue to move away from Expressionism, with its influence only really remaining in his use of lighting. In the most famous sequence of the film, for example, in which Tartüff, played brilliantly by Jannings, goes to Elmire to have his way with her, all we see of the man is his larger than life shadow in the light cast when he opens the door to her room - a great piece of chiaroscuro. Also, as the housekeeper goes to get the husband, shadows are again used to great effect as she furtively wanders up and down the huge staircase in the house with nothing but a candle to guide her. The whole sequence is, as Eisner puts it 'a real symphony of lighting effects.'

Subtext: The message of this film is, on one level, very simplistic. As the opening intertitle tells us, hypocrisy is everywhere. The world of Molière and seventeenth-century France is still relevant in the Weimar Germany of the 1920s. However, Kracauer, in his analysis, has the same complaint of this film as he has of *Caligari*, namely that the framing device was an unnecessary addition, and that the film doesn't actually say anything. For Kracauer it is all form and no content and is ultimately more concerned with its cinematography and the grand architecture of the Count's house than with forcing the spectator to question hypocrisy. I have to agree with Elsaesser, who challenges Kracauer's view. Elsaesser reveals the psychological depths of Murnau and Mayer's portrayal, showing how the characters of Tartüff, the Count and his wife do not necessarily have to be seen as a conman, a victim and a saviour respectively. Elsaesser suggests that Tartüff could be read not as a farcical character, but as a tragic, elemental figure who is driven to destruction by his own urges. The Count becomes a 'gutless and impotent pedant' and the wife a '"subconscious" seductress.' The duel nature of the characters revealed by Elsaesser thus makes far more complex (and therefore more interesting) the representation of hypocrisy in the film.

Verdict: There is some great acting in this film and the final sequence is very well constructed, but it's not up there with *Der letzte Mann*. 3/5

Faust (1926)

Cast: Eric Barclay (Duke of Parma), Hans Brausewetter (Farmboy), William Dieterle (Valentin: Gretchen's Brother), Gösta Ekman (Faust), Werner Fuetterer (Archangel), Yvette Guilbert (Marthe Schwerdtlein: Gretchen's Aunt), Camilla Horn (Gretchen), Emil Jannings (Mephisto), Lothar Müthel (Friar), Hanna Ralph (Duchess of Parma), Frida Richard (Gretchen's Mother)

Crew: Director F.W. Murnau, Writers Hans Kyser, Johann Wolfgang Goethe and Christopher Marlowe, Producer Erich Pommer, Cinematography Carl Hoffmann, Production Design Robert Herlth and Walter Röhrig, Ufa

Story: The devil is riding across the night sky, but is stopped by an angel. "Let me pass" cries the devil. The Earth is his to travel across and do with as he will. The angel refuses to accept this. Mankind belongs to God. The devil then proceeds to make the angel a wager. The pair agree that if he can turn a human heart away from God he will be given the Earth. Faust the elderly scholar is chosen as the guinea pig.

The devil starts by infecting Faust's town with the plague. Desperate to find a cure, Faust calls up the devil who appears to him in the guise of the wily Mephisto. If Faust will give him his soul Mephisto will grant his every

wish. At first Faust is nervous, so Mephisto gives him the chance of try
out the pact for one day. This Faust does. He saves the town, but does n
wish to remain in league with the devil. So Mephisto tempts Faust further,
giving him back his youth and allowing him to have the most beautiful
woman in Italy, the Countess of Parma. Faust is now unable to resist and so
he seals the pact for all eternity.

Soon Faust grows bored of indulging his every wish and becomes more
and more dissatisfied. Eventually he asks Mephisto to take him home. Here
he meets the beautiful, pure-hearted Gretchen, with whom he immediately
falls in love. Mephisto tries to discourage the relationship but Faust will not
change his mind. So Mephisto arranges for Gretchen and Faust to spend the
night together. However, while the couple are enjoying each other's company Mephisto informs Gretchen's brother, who rushes back to his sister's
home and finds Faust there. He attacks Faust with his sword and as Faust
attempts to defend himself, the brother is fatally wounded by Mephisto.
Faust escapes, and with his dying breath the brother tells the town that
Gretchen's lover has killed him. She is taken off to the stocks and from then
on treated as an outcast.

We next see Gretchen during winter. She has had a baby by Faust and
wanders the streets of the village looking for someone to take her in. She
finds no shelter and eventually collapses outside the town, where she is discovered by the town's guard and accused of leaving her baby for dead. She
is condemned to be burned at the stake and as the fire is built she calls out to
Faust. Faust hears her cries far away and demands that Mephisto take him to
his lover. Again Mephisto is reticent, but Faust insists and as the fire laps
around Gretchen, he joins her on the fire. In so doing he breaks the pacts
with the devil. Love conquers evil and the world is saved from the devil.

Background: This was Murnau's final project before he left for America
and like Lang's *Die Nibelungen* it can be seen as an attempt to make a specifically German epic. The writing of the film was fraught with difficulties.
Based on the plays by Marlowe and Goethe a first draft was produced by
Hans Kyser. However, Ufa didn't like it and so commissioned Gerhard
Hauptmann, the most important living writer of the time, to produce a new
script. Hauptmann refused to use Goethe and Marlowe as a basis, wanting
to create a completely new version. This he did, but again Ufa didn't like it,
feeling that his intertitles were too complicated. So eventually they decided

se Kyser's titles and put Hauptmann's work in the programme that was ⏺oduced for the film's premiere.

As with Murnau's other films, it's the cinematography that still impresses the spectator today. Visually, this film is very powerful. The perfect framing of the high-angled shot of the wild-eyed priest calling on his congregation to repent to protect themselves from the plague makes you realise that Murnau was a trained painter. Another sequence worthy of attention is the famous magic carpet ride of Mephisto and Faust. Here we see another fine example of the 'unchained camera' which follows Faust's gaze looking at the countryside rushing past.

This film sees Murnau return to a more overtly Expressionistic aesthetic than in *Tartüff*, for example. Chiaroscuro lighting is used throughout the film and the houses are reminiscent of *Der Müde Tod*. However, like in Lang's work, Murnau is not afraid to introduce farce into his tragedy. Jannings' show-stopping performance as Mephisto, the scheming devil who attempts to bring Faust to his doom, is hilarious at times, particularly in the scene where he playfully flirts with Gretchen's aunt to make her fall in love with him.

Subtext: The power of this film is, without a doubt, its visual splendour. As a performance of the Faust story it can hardly be said to do justice to either Marlowe's or Goethe's version of the story. These earlier versions explore the psychological turmoil of a man torn apart by ambition on the one hand and the wish to find contentment on the other. These plays are magnificently crafted both in terms of their dramatic structure and their use of language. However, although Murnau's film is visually brilliant, it loses much of the poetry, particularly of Goethe's version, and the depths of Faust's despair as he wrestles with the two sides of his nature are only ever hinted at in the broody performance of the Swedish actor Gösta Ekman. However, as a piece of melodrama it is at times moving, particularly towards the end of the film when the plight of Gretchen can't help but pull at the spectator's heart strings.

Verdict: Some of the best visual sequences to be found in German film, but I think they could have done more with the story. 4/5

4. Georg Wilhelm Pabst (1885-1967)

G.W. Pabst was born into a lower middle-class Austrian family. He grew up in Vienna and in 1901 entered the Vienna Conservatory to study acting. He worked throughout Austria and Germany and in 1911 went to the German *Volkstheater* in New York, where he eventually made the transition to directing. In 1914 as he attempted to return home, war broke out and so he was interned for the duration in France. After the War he returned to Vienna, where in 1921 he joined the Carl Froelich film company. In 1923 he directed his first movie, *Der Schatz/The Treasure*, a pedestrian film which nonetheless points the way thematically towards Pabst's later work in its examination of the explosive mixture of sex, money and power. In 1925 he had his first success with *Die freudlose Gasse/The Joyless Street*. However, this film didn't have an easy ride to the cinema, since it, like many of his subsequent movies, was plagued by problems of censorship. *Die freudlose Gasse* was then quickly followed by his first Ufa film, *Geheimnisse einer Seele/Secrets Of A Soul* (1926). In 1928 he helped to found the left-wing *Volks-Film-Verband*, two years later making his first talkie *Westfront 1918*, through which he got the name 'Red Pabst.' He also started working at this time on *Die Dreigroschenoper/The Threepenny Opera*, which was based on a musical by Brecht with whom he initially collaborated until the two men fell out. After a brief stay in Paris Pabst moved to Hollywood, making his first film for Warner Brothers, *A Modern Hero*, in 1933. But the director was not comfortable with the American style of working and so in 1936 he returned to France. As the Second World War approached Pabst decided to give America another go. His passage was booked for 8 September 1939. War broke out on 1 September, and so he was stuck in Nazi Germany. From 1939-1945 he made a number of successful films, but after the War the fact that he had stayed and worked in Germany hindered his career and in the 1950s his films never achieved the heights of the pre-war days. In 1957 he contracted Parkinson's Disease which brought his film-making career to an end. Pabst is the last of the 'big three' directors of the Weimar Period. He is generally acknowledged as the key figure in the 'street realism' which began to take over from Expressionism. But, as we shall see, although he is the least influenced by the earlier films of Wiene and Leni, he does not completely escape the clutches of *Caligari*'s legacy.

Die freudlose Gasse/The Joyless Street (1925)

Cast: Greta Garbo (Grete Rumfort), Asta Nielsen (Maria Lechner), Henry Stuart (Egon Stirner), Robert Garrison (Don Alfonso Canez), Valeska Gert (Mrs Greifer), Tamara Tolstoi (Lia Leid), Werner Krauss (Butcher of Melchior Street), Mario Cusmich (Colonel Irving), Agnes Esterhazy (Regina Rosenow), Karl Etlinger (Max Rosenow), Jaro Fürth (Hofrat Rumfort), Ilka Grüning (Mrs Rosenow), Einar Hanson (Lieutenant Davis), Max Kohlhase (Maria's Father), Krafft-Raschig (American Soldier), Edna Markstein (Mrs Merkel), Alexander Murski (Dr Leid), Loni Nest (Rosa Rumfort), Raskatoff (Trebitsch), Sylvia Torf (Maria's Mother), Hertha von Walther (Else)

Crew: Director G.W. Pabst, Writer Willy Haas, Novel Hugo Bettauer, Cinematography Robert Lach, Curt Oertel, Guido Seeber Production Design Otto Erdmann and Hans Sohnle

Story: The film focuses on the decline of three women living through the hard times of post-war Vienna on Melchior Street, in a run-down area of the city. Grete is the daughter of Hofrat Rumfort, a once well-to-do civil servant. She works as a secretary in an office where she is sexually harassed by her boss and ridiculed by her colleagues for wearing old clothes. Maria lives with her brutal parents who treat her as an unpaid skivvy. She dreams of a life with her handsome lover Egon Stirner. Else is the poorest of the three. She, her husband and baby are penniless and haven't even got a real place to live. Her decline is the quickest. At the beginning of the film we see her and her family squatting in a stable. As she hunts for food to feed her baby she is forced to prostitute herself with the butcher (played brilliantly by Werner Krauss) for a meagre piece of meat. Maria, who happened to be with Else in the butcher's but who refused the man's advances, is soon faced once again with the prospect of prostitution. Unwilling to carry on living at home, she goes to Egon and begs him to take her away. Egon has other plans. Whilst carrying on a relationship with Else, he is also attempting to marry a rich heiress, Regina Rosenow. To win her he needs to make a bit of money himself. All he needs is 100 Dollars so that he can make a fortune on the stock exchange. He tells Maria that he needs some cash and, eager to please him, she says that she'll get it. She goes to Mrs Greifer, a dressmaker, money-lender and (most importantly) landlady of a seedy nightclub, who takes her into her parlour. Here she is spotted by one of the club's regulars, Don Alfonso Canez, who takes an instant liking to her and leads her off to a secluded hotel to have his way with her. As he is wooing her, Maria hears a noise in another room. She looks through a window, only to see Egon, her true love (or so she thought), being given some pearls by Lia Leid, a rich married woman he has also asked to help him get some cash and who is clearly expecting something in return. Maria is overcome with rage and when Egon leaves the room she sneaks in and strangles her rival.

Back at Grete's things are not going well. Her father has lost all his money on the stock exchange and she has lost her job for refusing the advances of her boss. They decide to rent out a room and as luck would have it, a charming American officer takes it, paying Grete sixty dollars rent, a sum that is well over the odds. Then, just when things seem to be going okay again, Grete's little sister steals some food from the officer. He does not particularly mind, but the father is indignant when the American points out the theft, accusing the man of lying and kicking him out of the house. Also, Grete has to give all the money that they received from the officer to one of her father's creditors (something that she decides to keep from her father, so as not to worry him). Consequently the family is destitute and Grete now too goes to Mrs Greifer, who is more than willing to help, provided the girl is 'nice' to some of her customers.

Meanwhile the hunt has begun for Lia's killer. Maria seems to have lost all her former qualms and has become Canez's mistress. Eager to take revenge on her two-timing lover, she takes Canez back to the room where she heard Egon making love to the woman and tells her new lover she knows who Lia's killer was - Egon Stirner! Being a man of some influence Canez not only has Egon arrested but also manages to keep his mistress' name out of it. Maria's revenge would seem to be complete. But, as time wears on she becomes wracked with remorse, eventually being forced by her conscience to go to the police and admit her guilt. Egon is proved innocent. However, he has learnt his lesson and before he leaves Maria to her fate, the couple forgive each other.

Grete is now working, albeit unwillingly, for Mrs Greifer. She meets the men, but refuses to sleep with them. As she struggles with one particularly persistent guest she stumbles across the American who was living with them. He is at the club to investigate the seedy side of life in Vienna and is disgusted to find that the lovely Grete is a working girl, especially because he has just given her sixty dollars. He walks away, but just at that moment Grete's father turns up at Mrs Greifer's. He has found out that his daughter is being forced to degrade herself because of his debts. He explains why she is there to the officer who now decides to save her from Greifer and take her home.

Finally we return to Else. She too has moved to a room—in Mrs Greifer's. Her family are still starving and so once again she goes to the butcher's for food. But this time he won't give her anything—whatever she does. In desperation she forces herself into the shop. The next thing we see is the butcher at the shop window—covered in blood and dying. Else runs in panic back to her family. Meanwhile all hell has broken loose outside the club. The hungry masses out on the street have decided to attack to rich guests of the nightclub. In the chaos a fire breaks out in the club. As smoke fills their room the couple manage to pass their baby out of a window to the crowd below. But they cannot get out and are consumed by the flames.

Background: This was Pabst's second film and his first international hit. It was also the first and last German film made by Greta Garbo, although the real star of the film at the time was fellow Scandinavian Asta Nielsen, a woman who can be considered the first real international cinema star. The film is perhaps the most famous example of 'street realism' and can be seen as evidence of a more general trend in German culture away from Expressionism toward what became known as *Neue Sachlichkeit* or *New Objectivity*. That said, the film still bears the marks of the expressionist legacy. Firstly it is completely made in the studio, giving the 'realism' a theatrical feel. Secondly, Pabst isn't beyond throwing in some expressionist shadows every now and again to heighten the tension (have a look, for example, at the moment when the detectives searching for the murderer are walking down the stairs of the hotel).

But there is clearly a shift in this film towards a form of social realism not found in the films of Lang or Murnau. We see the same 'entfesselte' camera technique we find in *Der letzte Mann* but here, rather than giving the spectator the subjective perspective of an individual character, it gives the film the sense of being an objective documentary, a good example of this being the shot of crowds waiting outside the butcher's shop at night. As the camera pans along the queue, lighting up individual faces in turn, you almost forget for a moment you are watching a fictional film. The documentary realism is then contrasted with the melodrama of the narrative, as well as Pabst's sophisticated use of continuity editing, a technique which hides the joins in shots and which is now a standard element of mainstream narrative cinema.

A final point to mention here is the fact that most critics, when writing about the film base their analysis on a very sub-standard print. As a result they tend to see it as the story of Maria and Grete. However, recent restoration work has revealed a much more ambitious film which includes the story of Else (mentioned in my outline) as well as the story of Regina, although this final aspect of the film is still only really hinted at in the longest version currently available and so doesn't figure in my synopsis.

Subtext: The overwhelming trait of *New Objectivity* was a critical but resigned view of a society in crisis, a world-view clearly to be found in *Die freudlose Gasse*. The rich industrialists of Vienna are shown to be evil manipulators of the masses and in particular of women, who they buy at will. The original film, it would appear, was to show the treatment of women by men throughout society, as is suggested by the four women from different social classes who were to be its focus. However, the version we have mainly examines the middle and working classes. In particular, the film highlights the naked economic reality of prostitution, showing that even the apparently morally pure middle classes (embodied in the character of Grete) will, at least potentially, sell themselves if they fall on hard times.

Yet, while the social message of the film is clear, you can't help thinking that Pabst is treading a thin line between edification and titillation in some of the more risqué shots of Mrs Greifer's bar and the semi-naked girls who work there. The content of the film was considered too shocking in many European countries and was banned in Britain. Elsewhere it was greatly cut, hence the version we have being in such bad shape. The social message of the film is also, it must be said, tempered by Pabst's use of melodrama, particularly in the stories of Grete, which ultimately undermine the social realism. Grete, of course, never does prostitute herself. As a result the film seems to suggest that the morally virtuous can escape the clutches of a life of depravity since Grete is finally saved by her twentieth-century knight in shining armour - an American officer.

Verdict: Although this isn't strictly speaking an expressionist film, it has to be included in any survey of the period. Firstly, it is a classic of the new realism which came out of the earlier movement. Secondly, although still very young at the time, the film captures the magnificence of Garbo, definitely pointing towards the star she was to become. The only real weakness in the film is its tendency towards melodrama, which takes the edge off the reality of prostitution. Nevertheless, worth watching. 4/5

Geheimnisse einer Seele/Secrets Of A Soul (1926)

Cast: Renata Brausewetter (Servant Girl), Ilka Grüning (The Mother), Werner Krauss (Martin Fellman), Pawel Pawloff (Dr Orth), Jack Trevor (Erich), Ruth Weyher (His Wife), Hertha Von Walther (Fellman's Assistant)

Crew: Director G.W. Pabst, Writers Karl Abraham, Hans Neumann, Colin Ross, Hanns Sachs, Cinematography Robert Lach, Curt Oertel, Guido Seeber, Production Design Ernö Metzner

Story: A happily married professor of chemistry is disturbed whilst he is shaving by someone screaming for help. It turns out that one of his neighbours has been murdered with a razor. The same day he finds out that his wife's cousin and childhood friend is returning home after years of foreign travel. That night the professor is plagued by a series of terrible nightmares in which he is shot by his wife's cousin, who then pops up again as his wife's lover and the father of her child. The dream ends with the man desperately stabbing a ghostly apparition of his wife. The next day, he begins to be taken over by a profound fear of knives. The cousin arrives, but the professor is unable even to eat dinner and rushes out of the house, much to his wife's dismay.

We next see the man sitting in a pub, thinking about what to do next. As he leaves, he forgets his key. Luckily a kindly doctor spots his mistake and follows him. He gives back the key, telling the man that he realises he is troubled and that it is his job to help people like him. Thinking nothing more of this meeting the man goes into his house. Here he is greeted by his wife. She tries to comfort him but as she holds him he grabs a knife from the table and almost stabs her.

Shocked by his behaviour he rushes out of the house again, this time to his mother. "Is there nobody he knows who can help him?" she asks. The man remembers the person from the pub whom he discovers is a psychoanalyst. The film then plots the man's course of therapy. He stays with his mother for the next few months and has regular meetings with the doctor, who gradually digs deeper and deeper into the causes of the man's phobia. We learn that although he is happily married, the couple are frustrated because they have no children. Finally, the man is taken back to his childhood, through which he comes to realise that he has always been jealous of his wife's close relationship with her cousin. Both these frustrations then erupted as a knife phobia after the shock of the neighbour's murder.

Now that he at last understands the roots of his problem, he can overcome it and return to his wife. After they are reunited (the cousin having left), we are shown an epilogue, in which the couple are on holiday in the countryside, and miraculously at last seem to have managed to have a child. At last their lives are complete.

Background: Originally this film was to be an educational film, outlining the main principles of Freudian psychoanalysis, but Freud never really trusted the cinema as a medium and so refused to cooperate. But Ufa did manage to get two members of Freud's inner sanctum to collaborate on the script and the film was premiered at Freud's 70th birthday celebrations in Berlin. On the one hand, this film continues to use elements of documentary-style realism in its attempt to give an objective, dispassionate account of one man's recovery from mental illness. On the other, the film can be seen as one of the last to use overt expressionist style, a style which is confined wholly to the extraordinary dream sequence in which the man's subconscious fears are communicated through a montage of abstract images, such as a collage of laughing faces, or a peal of bells which turn into women's faces which are intercut with shots of the man sleeping fitfully. Abstraction is also used in the therapy sequences, where the man replays events from the past in his mind and which are shot against a white background to make it clear to the spectator that they are being imagined. Like *Die freudlose Gasse*, the film had a hard time with the censor and was felt to be too sexually explicit but the print that survives is more complete than the earlier film. The only scene which appears to be missing is one in which the man goes to his laboratory to contemplate suicide before he decides to go to his mother's. One overlooked film connection is worth mentioning here. As I've already said, Luis Buñuel was highly influenced by Lang, but the opening sequence of *Geheimnisse einer Seele*, in which we see the man sharpening his razor on a strop, staring into the shaving mirror and then going over to his wife to cut her hair strongly recalls the opening of *Un chien andalou* (1929). Although in the later film it's not the woman's hair that gets cut with the man's razor but her eyeball.

Subtext: The ambitious aim of the film to provide the spectator an overview of Freud's theories is not really achieved here. Instead we're given a rather superficial, cod version of psychoanalysis and in particular the interpretation of dreams. The Doctor in the film carefully explains the symbolic importance of each aspect. Here we see the subconscious forces implicitly examined in other films we have discussed writ large. We return to those old favorites - Eros and Thanatos. Sex and death are once again seen as two sides of the same coin, the man's jealous desire for his wife manifesting itself in an urge to murder her. The superficiality of the film's use of Freud is then confirmed in the tacked-on epilogue, in which we see the couple now with the baby they have always longed for, an end so laden with schmaltz that it almost totally undermines the documentary objectivity Pabst is trying to construct.

Verdict: An interesting film from an historical point of view. Not his best. 2/5

Die Liebe der Jeanne Ney/
The Love Of Jeanne Ney (1927)

Cast: Edith Jehanne (Jeanne Ney), Uno Henning (Andreas Labov), Fritz Rasp (Khalibiev), Brigitte Helm (Gabrielle), Adolf E. Licho (Raymond Ney), Eugen Jensen (Andre Ney), Hans Jaray (Poitras), Siegfried Arno (Gaston), Hertha von Walther (Margot), Vladimir Sokoloff (Zacharkiewicz)

Crew: Director G.W. Pabst, Writers Rudolf Leonhardt and Ladislaus Vajda, Novel Ilja Ehrenburg, Cinematography Robert Lach and Fritz Arno Wagner, Editing G.W. Pabst and Marc Sorkin, Production Design Otto Hunte and Victor Trivas

Story: We are in a town in the Crimea during the Russian Civil War, a town which is run by decadent White Russians and corrupt opportunists.

The evil Khalibiev decides to make a few quick Rubles by selling a list Bolshevik spies operating locally to a member of the French Embassy who along with his daughter, the film's heroine, Jeanne, are just about to escape to France. Before they can leave, the Bolsheviks find out about their betrayal and send a couple of comrades to recover the list. In the struggle the man is shot dead. Jeanne, hearing the shot, comes into her father's room. She sees the men who have done this terrible deed and is shocked to discover that one of them is Andreas, a revolutionary she first met in Russia and with whom she had a brief affair. He warns her to escape; the Bolsheviks are about to take the town. She cannot leave in time and is captured by the victorious army. But Andreas, with the help of his contacts amongst the Reds, manages to get her passage home. We next see Jeanne in Paris with her uncle Raymond, who runs a detective agency. Although he is at first rather reticent about taking her in, his blind daughter Gabrielle is overjoyed at her cousin's return and insists that she stays. Meanwhile, Khalibiev has realised that things are not going his way in the Crimea and so he too decides to go to France. While he was in Jeanne's father's office he had noticed a letter that the man was writing to his brother telling of his and his daughter's imminent return. Once he arrives in Paris, he decides to concoct a story to ingratiate himself with this man. In the uncle's office he sees both the uncle's daughter and the money in his safe. His next move seems obvious. He will declare his love for the daughter, marry her, gain access to the father's cash and then get rid of her. Whilst this is all going on, Andreas also turns up in Paris. He has been sent by the Bolsheviks to try and provoke revolution amongst the sailors of Toulon. He makes contact with Jeanne and now away from the war in Russia, the couple feel that they can perhaps build a life together.

But Khalibiev has other ideas. His plans to marry Gabrielle have gone awry. He has told Margot, a beautiful barmaid with whom he promises to run away once he has got rid of his wife, what he intends to do. Margot is disgusted by the plan and immediately goes to Gabrielle to warn her off. Meanwhile, Gabrielle's father has had a bit of luck. His agency has managed to recover a lost diamond and so has earned a $50,000 reward. As Raymond waits in a frenzy for the money, Khalibiev comes to the agency. Having been rejected by both the father and his daughter he has decided to come back to steal the diamond. He kills Raymond and in the process man-s to frame Andreas by leaving his picture. Jeanne is distraught when she arns that her lover is a suspect in her uncle's murder. Yet all is not lost. Andreas has an alibi. He was with Jeanne, the couple having spent a night in a hotel to consummate their relationship. Even more luckily, there was a witness. By chance, Khalibiev had also been there. He will be able to prove that Andreas didn't commit the crime. Jeanne goes to Khalibiev's hotel, but when he sees her he jumps in a taxi and heads for the train station to escape. Jeanne manages to catch the same train. She pleads with Khalibiev to come with her to the police. He only agrees to do this if he can have his way with her. Initially she accepts this deal but as he makes his advances she is disgusted. They struggle; Jeanne pulls the communication cord and in the chaos he loses his grip on the diamond. Now Jeanne realises that Khalibiev is her uncle's murderer. He tries to escape the train but is caught by the guards and, in her mind's eye, Jeanne is finally reunited forever with her lover.

Background: This film continues Pabst's examination of life in the aftermath of World War One. However, as Kracauer points out, this time it's on a much grander scale. 'This time, the plot, instead of involving a single European capital, encompassed virtually the whole of European post-war society, including Soviet Russia.' The look at life in the Crimea was, to a large extent, a result of the success of Eisenstein's *Battleship Potemkin*, released the previous year. What the Ufa bosses wanted was a Russian film but to ensure mass success (Ufa was still reeling from the expense of *Metropolis*) it was to be shot in an 'American style.' By this they meant that Pabst wasn't to use Eisenstein's abstract montage editing, in which shots are placed next to each other for their symbolic meaning. To a degree this is what Pabst did. Although editing for Pabst is as important as it is for Eisenstein (the brief three-minute sequence in which Khalibiev sees the list of Bolsheviks has forty different shots Iris Barry informs us), his purpose is to construct a seamless, realist narrative. *Jeanne Ney* probably has the most sophisticated continuity editing of any film of its day.

We also see here the continuation of Pabst's quasi documentary style, his roving camera once again being used to construct the illusion of realism, a realism augmented here by his use of real locations and non-professional actors for some of the scenes. Kenneth MacPherson claims, for example, that for the sequence in which we see a group of White Russians having an

orgy, Pabst simply got together 120 Russian officers, provided them w
drink and women and shot what happened.

Yet, as with *Die freudlose Gasse*, Expressionism is not completely for-
gotten. Indeed, there are echoes of Murnau's work here (not surprisingly
perhaps given Pabst's use of Fritz Arno Wagner). This is particularly appar-
ent in the scene of Raymond's murder. We are reminded perhaps of *Nosferatu* as we see the shadow of Khalibiev approaching Raymond's office. Also
his use of high and low angled camera shots attempt at times to disorient the
spectator and gestures towards a representation of the psychological inner
world of the characters which dominated many of the films of the first flush
of Expressionism. However, this undermines the film's attempt to construct
a completely objective view of the world.

Subtext: Although Pabst doesn't really follow Eisenstein's editing technique, he does sympathise with his politics. David Bathrick claims, for
example, that before making *Jeanne Ney*, he had joined two left-wing film
organisations, The German Worker's Film Syndicate and the Volks-Film-
Verband. He goes on to suggest that the filming of *Jeanne Ney* was therefore fortuitous for both Ufa, who could cash in on the success of *Potemkin*,
and for Pabst who was able to tell a story about the Russian revolution and
to portray the Bolsheviks in a sympathetic light. We also see in the film a
strong impulse to contextualise the actions of the characters, showing in
great detail the nature of their environment (as we see, most famously, in
the opening shot of Khalibiev which moves from his boots up his body,
focusing on the squalor that surrounds him). But the realism of the film is,
once again, undermined by Pabst's use of melodrama. In *Potemkin* the story
refuses to focus on a set of individuals, giving rather an image of the revolution of 1905. In *Jeanne Ney* the events in Russia and the rest of Europe ultimately become the backdrop for a romantic crime story in which the purity
of women - both Jeanne and Gabrielle (played by Brigitte Helm, who
returns to the role of the paragon of beauty and innocence she portrayed so
well in *Metropolis*) - triumphs over the evil villain. The realist credentials of
the film would further seem to be undermined by the changes made to the
Ilja Ehrenburg novel, in which, for example, Jeanne's lover does not escape
and she is forced to succumb to the advances of Khalibiev. Ehrenburg was
very annoyed by what had been done to his work. He publicly attacked it,
claiming that (as Bathrick quotes) 'In my book ... life is badly organised,

69

efore it has to be changed. In the film, life is well organised, therefore .e can go home to bed.'

Verdict: That said, the film cannot be dismissed for being a melodrama. This is one of Pabst's most consummate piece of editing. Its story, whilst conventional is nonetheless gripping and it is not without its critique of bourgeois life (have a look, for example at the uncle's descent into madness at the prospect of getting the $50,000—a clear attack on the system of values under capitalism). 4/5

Die Büchse der Pandora/Pandora's Box (1929)

Cast: Louise Brooks (Lulu), Fritz Kortner (Dr Schön), Francis Lederer (Alwa Schön), Carl Goetz (Schigolch), Krafft-Raschig (Rodrigo Quast), Alice Roberts (Countess Anna Geschwitz), Gustav Diessl (Jack the Ripper), Sig Arno (Instructor), Daisy D'Ora (Charlotte M.A. von Zanik), Michael von Newlinsky (Marquis Casti-Piani)

Crew: Director G.W. Pabst, Writers Joseph Fleisler, G.W. Pabst, Ladislaus Vajda, Plays Frank Wedekind, Producer Seymour Nebenzal, Cinematography Günther Krampf, Production Design Andrej Andrejew and Gottlieb Hesch

Story: Lulu is a woman of outstanding beauty that no man (or indeed woman) can resist. At the start of the film she is the mistress of Schön, a media tycoon, who puts her up in a flash penthouse. However, Schön is not the only visitor to Lulu's flat. Enter Schigolch, a disgusting drunk who lives off handouts from Lulu and who is introduced to Schön as her first protector. Schigolch has a proposition for Lulu. He claims that the world should know of her beauty, that she should take to the stage with a colleague of his, Rodrigo. But Schön has a better idea. He convinces his son to give Lulu the lead in his song and dance show. Lulu is ecstatic, but her happiness is soon swept away. Schön informs Lulu that he is to marry and that he must end his affair. Lulu will not accept his decision. He brings his wife to be to the opening night of the show. When she sees the other woman Lulu flies into a rage, refusing to take the stage. Schön is called to her and as he orders her to go on she sulks like a child, demanding that he come back to her. Eventually he is unable to resist her charms. They kiss and at that very moment Schön's wife to be turns up and sees the couple embracing. Lulu has achieved her

aim. The wedding is off. Schön now realises that he will never escape L.
and so he accepts his fate, as if he were accepting a death sentence, and mar
ries her. At the wedding, the sense that Schön is heading towards his own
destruction overcomes the man. Pulling out a gun, he begs Lulu to kill herself so that they might both be free. She refuses and as they struggle the gun
goes off and Schön is killed.

We next see Lulu dressed in widow's weeds on trial for her husband's
murder. Although the defence makes an impassioned plea for her innocence
and even calls upon Schön's son as a witness (he is also in love with her),
the jury find her guilty. Before she can be led away Alwa sets off the fire
alarm and Lulu escapes in the chaos. She rushes back to Schön's house,
where she meets Alwa again and begs him to help her. He cannot resist her
and so organises their, as well as Schigolch and Rodrigo's, escape to Paris.
On the train they are recognised by a man who offers them help by putting
them up on a secluded gambling ship he knows of. Here they spend the next
three months.

By now things are beginning to go sour. Alwa has apparently gambled
away all their cash and Rodrigo is starting to turn nasty, ordering Lulu to
'get' 20,000 Francs so that he can set up his own vaudeville show. The only
hope on the horizon is the arrival of the Countess Geschwitz, a close friend
of Lulu. It becomes almost immediately clear that Geschwitz feels a great
deal more than friendship for the woman. She too has fallen for Lulu's
charms. However, Lulu's moment of happiness is almost immediately shat-
tered. Now Alwa has run out of money, the owner of the gambling ship has
no reason to keep Lulu. He could simply turn her over to the police and get
the reward but he has had a more lucrative offer from an Egyptian brothel
owner who wants to buy her for his place in Cairo.

Getting desperate, Lulu borrows money from Geschwitz which she gives
to Alwa. In a final attempt to recoup his losses he cheats at cards but is discovered before he can collect his winnings. A riot breaks out in the gambling hall. Alwa runs away and in the mêlée Lulu and Schigolch escape.

We next see Alwa, Lulu and Schigolch living a pitiful existence in London during the height of Jack the Ripper's reign of terror. It is Christmas
time, Alwa and Schigolch are doing nothing. Although Schigolch in particular always seems to be able to get whiskey, he can never apparently find
any food. What he wants more than anything is to taste Christmas pudding.

Lulu goes out to earn some money on the streets. In a cruel twist of fate he picks up Jack the Ripper but even he would not seem to be able to resist her charms. As she stares into his eyes the man is overcome with emotion and drops the knife concealed behind his back. She takes him back to his room where the couple embrace. As he holds her he eyes a knife glistening on the table next to him which he grabs - the rest is inevitable. Lulu is dead. In the last shot of the film we see Schigolch sitting in a bar, tucking into a large Christmas pudding.

Background: This is undoubtedly Pabst's most famous film, although when it was first released it was slammed by critics. The film has reached classic status, due in no small part to the American actress Louise Brooks' performance as Lulu. The film shot Brooks to stardom, putting her for a brief period of time on a par with the likes of Joan Crawford. But the stardom didn't last and after a brief spell in Europe working with Pabst she returned to Hollywood where she only managed to get bit parts. She made her final film *Overland Stage Raiders* with John Wayne in 1938, after which she faded into obscurity until *Die Büchse der Pandora* was revived in 1955 in Paris by Henri Langlois at the Musée National d'Art Moderne. This exhibition was dominated by huge posters of Brooks as Lulu. The enthusiasm for the actress and the film aroused by the exhibition gave birth to what has become today a Louise Brooks cult. With her perfectly formed black bob, and childlike innocence Brooks as Lulu has become, along with Marlene Dietrich, a central icon of the Weimar period, the femme fatale, a symbol of the loose morality of the roaring 1920s - curiously, Dietrich was up for the role, until Pabst vetoed the choice. Brooks acts very naturally in the film - the antithesis of the exaggerated performances we see in most Expressionist films. The turn towards realism continues, but as we have already seen in Pabst's other films, there is still the thumbprint of Expressionism here, most obviously in his use of chiaroscuro lighting and sharp camera angles, but also in the film's subtext.

Subtext: Here we see echoed many of the themes already dealt with both in Pabst's work and the films of other artists we've been looking at. Most obviously, we see an exploration of the fear of female sexuality discussed in Lang's *Metropolis*. While on trial the prosecution compares Lulu to the figure of Pandora from Greek mythology who unleashed disaster and destruction into the world. On one level, Lulu is constructed in the film not so much as a woman but as a mythical force who destroys everyone wh comes into her path. Like the evil Maria, she can be seen as evidence of the destructive power of liberated sexuality and as in *Metropolis*, although Lulu would seem to be at the centre of the narrative, the film would seem to be more about male sexuality. Lulu is the ultimate passive aggressive, an idea which is communicated in Pabst's use of the gaze as a thematic strand of the film. Throughout the film she transfixes her conquests with her gaze. Although she might seem to control the various men she stares at, from Schön to Jack the Ripper, she only stares to invite others to stare at her. If we look at the end of the film and Lulu's encounter with Jack the Ripper, we seen a magnificent shot/reverse shot sequence between Jack and Lulu in which Pabst gradually zooms into the characters' eyes until finally Jack releases the knife. Throughout, Lulu's eyes communicate an innocence and her willingness to give herself to this man, a look which he finds irresistible.

Lulu is a catalyst for the unleashing of the male libido (even Geschwitz, a woman enamoured of Lulu, is clearly a 'masculine' lesbian). After her death we see Jack the Ripper (a figure which recalls Leni's *Das Wachsfigurenkabinett*) walk past Alwa, giving him a knowing glance, perhaps suggesting that he has ultimately done Alwa a good turn. The man is at last free of Lulu, Jack has resealed Pandora's box. But working against this image of Lulu as the destroyer of men is the social critique of the film, a critique which echoes Pabst's *Die freudlose Gasse*. As Geschwitz points out in the courtroom scene, Lulu, having been brought up on the streets, has no choice but to live the life she does. Lulu has nothing to offer but her body. As she slips down the social strata the naked economic reality of her position becomes more and more obvious. Her status as a femme fatale who can destroy men with her wiles disappears. On the gambling ship she is reduced to a commodity, sold against her will into slavery, and then finally in London she is reduced to the level of a street prostitute. The femme fatale is a victim of male society.

Verdict: Again Pabst shows himself to be a consummate editor, but this film is in a league of its own due to, as Eisner puts it, the 'miracle of Louise Brooks.' 5/5

5. The Coming Of Sound
And The Going Of Expressionism

By the time sound came on the scene things were beginning to change radically not only in German cinema, but also in German society as a whole. Clashes between right- and left-wing extremists were becoming more commonplace. Gradually, as the right wing began to dominate, many of Germany's most important actors, cameramen, producers, set designers and directors started to lose all hope in the future of the German film industry and the exodus to Hollywood, which had begun back in the early 1920s, became more widespread. Fritz Lang, Billy Wilder, Peter Lorre, to name but three, all made the journey to the States, bringing with them the styles and techniques they had learned on the sets of Weimar Germany, transferring the Angst of post-World War One Germany to post-Second World War America which was also gripped by social upheavals and its own forms of paranoia. Slowly the psychological abstraction of German Expressionism mutated into the seedy world of 1950s *Film Noir*.

Unfortunately there's no space to go into the next stage in the story of Expressionism here. If you want to explore this connection further have a look at Paul Duncan's Pocket Essential *Film Noir*. But before we leave Germany to be taken over by the Nazis, let's take a look at Weimar cinema's last years and three of the key talkies from the period. Although these films are very different from those of the early 1920s they, like the silent work of Pabst, can't completely escape the clutches of this earlier phase. However, what's particularly interesting is that in their mixture of Realism and Expressionism we can clearly see the beginnings of the *Noir* style to which so many big names of Weimar would eventually turn.

Der Blaue Engel/The Blue Angel (1930)

Cast: Emil Jannings (Prof. Immanuel Rath), Marlene Dietrich (Lola Lola), Kurt Gerron (Kiepert, the Magician), Rosa Valetti (Guste, his Wife), Hans Albers (Mazeppa, the Strong Man), Reinhold Bernt (The Clown), Eduard von Winterstein (Headmaster), Hans Roth (The Janitor), Rolf Müller (Pupil Angst), Carl Balhaus (Pupil Ertzum), Robert Klein-Lörk (Pupil Goldstaub), Charles Puffy (Innkeeper), Wilhelm Diegelmann (Captain), Gerhard Bienert (Policeman), Ilse Fürstenberg (Rath's Maid)

Crew: Director Josef von Sternberg, Writers Carl Zuckmayer, Karl Vollmöller, Heinrich Mann and Robert Liebmann, Novel Heinrich Mann, Producer Erich Pommer, Music Frederick Hollander, Cinematography Günther Rittau, Production Design Otto Hunte, Ufa

Story: Professor Rath, an arrogant buffoon of a man who teaches English at a local grammar school, is appalled to learn that some of his pupils are regulars at The Blue Angel, a nightclub in the seedy part of town. Here they are apparently spending their time with the star of the club's current cabaret act, Lola Lola, an erotic postcard of whom he finds circulating around the classroom. The Professor decides to go to the club to catch his pupils in the act. On his arrival he sees the boys and chases them into the star's dressing room, only to then have them escape. In the dressing room he meets the beautiful Lola and, just like his pupils, becomes immediately enamoured with the woman.

The following evening Rath returns to the club, ostensibly to pick up the hat he forgot the previous night. However, a hat is not all he picks up and he ends up spending the night with Lola. The same day he proposes to her, which (after she has stopped laughing) she accepts. The school is unable to accept the Professor's wish to marry Lola, so he is forced to leave but the Professor doesn't care. For the first time in his life he is truly happy, so much so that he crows like a cock on his wedding day. As Lola is getting changed after the wedding Rath stumbles upon the postcards that have been going around the school. Never will these postcards be sold, he declares, not as long as he has a single penny.

The film then cuts to a far more dishevelled image of the Professor who is now selling the postcards in the clubs where Lola performs. Time has passed and Rath has clearly come down in the world, working as a skivvy r his wife and as a clown in the cabaret - the cockcrowing which had so amused the people at the wedding now constitutes the central piece in his act. His humiliation reaches its climax when the troupe return to the Professor's home town and to The Blue Angel. In front of a packed house he is to re-enact his cockcrowing. Initially, he stands silently on the stage, refusing to perform. Then, as he looks backstage, he sees his wife in the arms of another man. He becomes deranged, crowing incessantly as he runs off stage. He smashes down the door to his wife's dressing room and starts to strangle her. Eventually he is pulled away and put in a straitjacket. After he has calmed down, the club manager takes pity on him and releases him. Rath puts on his hat and coat and scurries off to his old school, where he is later discovered by the caretaker, dead but still clinging to his old desk.

Background: At Emil Jannings' request Erich Pommer brought Joseph von Sternberg over from Hollywood to ensure international success for this joint Ufa/Paramount production, which was made in both German and English versions (the German version, however, is far superior). Born Josef Sternberg in Austria, he grew up in the States, where he was told to add the 'von' to his name to make himself sound more impressive. The film was to be a vehicle for Jannings, who gives an incredibly powerful performance as Professor Rath, but the limelight is stolen by Marlene Dietrich—or, more specifically, by her legs, which are always centre stage during Lola's act. Dietrich, a graduate of Max Reinhardt's theatre school, was discovered by Sternberg in a cabaret show and, against much opposition, he insisted on giving this relatively unknown actress the part of Lola Lola. In *Der Blaue Engel*, Sternberg moulded Dietrich into the husky-voiced femme fatale which was to become her trademark image. Afterwards, Sternberg brought Dietrich back to Hollywood with him, where she was marketed as Paramount's answer to MGM's Greta Garbo. For five years Sternberg was a Svengali figure to Dietrich. However, gradually their partnership broke down as Dietrich's success began to outstrip that of her old mentor.

Subtext: Although the film continues Weimar cinema's turn towards realism, the opening shot of the roofs of the town, crammed together and jutting out at different angles, looks like a more realistic version of the painted *mise en scène* of *Caligari*. Thematically too there are echoes of the earlier film, particularly in the use of the world of the cabaret, which can be seen as a reworking of the fairground motif in Wiene's *Caligari*. In *Der*

Blaue Engel the demi-monde setting of the cabaret turns the normal values of bourgeois society on their head to hold them up to ridicule. Professor Rath has always been a buffoon but while he is still a teacher he is able to hide his foolishness behind a mask of arrogant respectability. Once he becomes involved in the cabaret, however, the veneer of respectability is lost and his true self is revealed. On stage he performs, somewhat ironically, a much more authentic role than that of a middle-class teacher: he becomes the clown and object of public ridicule that he has really always been.

As in *Die Büchse der Pandora*, at the centre of the male protagonist's demise is a femme fatale. Like Brooks, there is a strong sense of androgyny at work in Dietrich's portrayal of Lola, making her a dangerously disturbing woman who seems to stand out from the crowd. Brooks' androgyny lies in the sense of boyish innocence she exudes. She seems to act without thinking, unaware of the power she holds. Dietrich, on the other hand, is very aware of her control over men, her masculine brand of femininity being overtly suggested in the song 'Falling in Love Again,' where her voice slips down an octave to sing the line "Men swarm around me like moths to a flame, if they get burnt it's not my fault." Here, she directly warns Rath that she will destroy him but knows at the same time that he, as a lustful male, has no choice but to yield to her hypnotic sexuality. However, as was the case in Pabst's film, the plot is not focused from the perspective of the femme fatale but solely through Rath's desiring male gaze. Lola may be the centre of attention but her own concerns and desires are peripheral to the plot. The character of Lola, in other words, only takes on substance and meaning when she is being looked at and desired by a man. It doesn't matter what she's singing about, just as long as she allows us to stare at her long, shapely legs, legs which embody her deadly sexual charms and which are shown off to a ridiculous extreme in her deliberately revealing skirt.

Verdict: Another must see, particularly for Dietrich fans. But Jannings' performance is also great, subtly poised between provoking bathos and pathos in the spectator. Wwatch out for the allusion to his performance in *Der letzte Mann* in the final sequence when the school caretaker finds him dead in the classroom. 4/5

Die Dreigroschenoper/The Threepenny Opera (1931)

Cast: Rudolf Forster (Mackie Messer), Carola Neher (Polly Peachum), Reinhold Schünzel (Tiger Brown), Fritz Rasp (Peachum), Valeska Gert (Mrs Peachum), Lotte Lenya (Jenny), Hermann Thimig (The Priest), Ernst Busch (The Street Singer), Vladimir Sokoloff (Smith, The Jailer), Paul Kemp, Gustav Püttjer, Oskar Höcker, Krafft-Raschig (Mackie Messer's Gang Members), Herbert Grünbaum (Filch)

Crew: Director G.W. Pabst, Writers Bertold Brecht, Béla Balázs, Léo Lania and Ladislaus Vajda, Producer Seymour Nebenzal, Music Kurt Weill, Cinematography Fritz Arno Wagner, Production Design Andrej Andrejew

Story: London at the turn of the last century. Enter Mackie Messer (Mack the Knife in English), a dandified master criminal in bowler hat and white gloves, who is walking out of a brothel. Here he has been enjoying the charms of Jenny the prostitute. As he says his fond farewell he is distracted by the beautiful Polly Peachum. He ditches Jenny and follows the other woman. The next thing we know, Mackie has proposed to Polly and is marshalling his gang to organise the wedding, no mean feat since this also involves robbing enough furniture for his bride's trousseau. The ceremony takes place that night in a deserted warehouse and who should appear at this top crime boss' celebration but Tiger Brown, the head of the police! It turns out that Mackie and Brown are old army buddies and we discover the secret of Mackie's success. As long as Brown is running Scotland Yard, Mackie can carry out his burglaries without any fear of being arrested.

The following morning, Polly returns home to her parents. We learn that her father is Mackie's only real rival in the city, since he controls all the beggars in London. No one can work here without his licence. Peachum is furious when he finds out what his daughter has done, claiming that she is a romantic fool for not seeing through Mackie. He decides he must save his daughter and so goes to the police. Of course Tiger Brown doesn't want to intervene against his friend. But Peachum has an ace up his sleeve. If Brown doesn't help him, Peachum will organise his beggars to disrupt the coronation which is to take place shortly, a disturbance which could cost Brown his job.

Polly rushes back to her husband to warn him about her father. At first Mackie won't believe her. Finally he accepts that things are serious so he

decides to flee, leaving his business in the hands of Polly, a decision wh.
is greeted with a good deal of derision by his gang. After a romantic fare
well, Polly returns to the gang, immediately stamping her authority on the
men and leaving them in no doubt that she is more than just a silly romantic
girl.

Rather than run away, Mackie decides to indulge in his usual weekly
visit to Jenny's brothel, even stopping to admire his own wanted poster on
the way. But while Mackie is being cocky about his chances of arrest, Mrs
Peachum is inside the brothel telling Jenny about the wedding to her daughter. Jenny is heartbroken and so agrees to betray her lover to the police when
he arrives. This she does but almost immediately regrets it since, when
Mackie arrives, he is his old charming self. Remorseful, Jenny warns him
that the police are coming and helps him escape. On his way out he meets
yet another woman who takes his fancy and decides to hide out with her for
a while. Deciding the coast is clear (and having finished making love to the
woman) he leaves her, only to run smack into the police and so he is taken
off to jail.

Meanwhile, Peachum is furious, thinking Mackie has escaped and so
makes up his mind to carry out the threat he made to Brown and to disturb
the coronation. The day of the coronation arrives and Peachum fires up his
beggars to go and disrupt events. But the film now takes a strange twist.
Things have changed within the gang under Polly's officious leadership.
Rather than continuing with burglary they have opened a bank, a far more
effective way of ripping off society. Mackie is now the bank president. Mrs
Peachum tells her husband the news and he immediately tries to call off the
demonstration. Mackie is now a man to be reckoned with and so is a perfect
match for his daughter. However, the beggars won't be calmed and so the
demonstration goes ahead.

Mackie breaks out of jail to take charge of the bank. With the beggars
rioting, Brown realises he is ruined and rides to the bank to look for his
friend, who promptly tells him not to worry and offers him a partnership in
the bank. Finally Peachum turns up in Mackie's office. Having experienced
the riot he now truly understands the power of the poor masses and so he
offers Mackie another partnership, between the bank's money and his influence with society's underclass. Together they can run everything. And so all
ends 'happily' with the three men working together for mutual benefit.

Background: Pabst's film is based on the hugely successful stage musical by Bertold Brecht and Kurt Weill. The Marxist playwright Brecht was one of the most important dramatists of the twentieth century, and was a central figure of the early German avant-garde, of which literary Expressionism was a key element. Rather than trying to write realistic plays, Brecht wrote what he termed 'Epic Theatre.' Central to this was his *Verfremdungseffekt*, or 'Defamiliarisation Effect.' By having his actors step out of character, or by using ironic captions to introduce episodes, he would never allow the audience to forget that they were watching a play and not real life. Through these techniques he hoped that he would provoke his audience into thinking more carefully about the events they had seen. *Die Dreigroschenoper* was Brecht's first big stage hit and the film his first foray into the world of movies. However, although initially collaborating in the writing of the screenplay both Brecht and Weill soon began to feel that the film was compromising their aesthetic and political intentions and so took the film company, Nero films, to court. A very public lawsuit ensued which saw Brecht eventually lose and Weill settle out of court.

The main difference between the film and the stage play is the use of realism, undermining the principles of 'Epic Theatre.' Also, Weill's beautifully grating songs, which provide a powerful commentary on the stage narrative, are kept to a minimum here and seem rather added on. That said, in its own right this is still an important film and it does manage to keep some of the feel of the stage play (indeed, some of the main characters are played by the same actors, including Kurt Weill's wife, Lotte Lenya as Jenny). Also, the street performer who sings the 'Ballad of Mac the Knife' (made famous in English by Louis Armstrong), sporadically addresses the audience directly to comment on the narrative and in so doing gestures towards Brecht's notion of 'Defamiliarisation.' In terms of film style, there is a degree of continuity with *Die Büchse der Pandora*. We see the same use of shadows, harking back, as Eisner points out, to the chiaroscuro lighting used during Expressionism. But particularly impressive in this film are Andrej Andrejew's sets, for which he constructed a huge, half-real, half-fantasy image of London at the turn of the last century, crammed with dark labyrinthine passages which again recall the Expressionistic world of Wiene and Leni.

Subtext: Die Dreigroschenoper is a satire on the nature of capitalism. In a sense it can be seen as a more radical version of *M* (a film clearly influenced by Brecht's play as can be seen in Lang's use of the beggars as spies), or as a comic reworking of *Dr Mabuse*. The central message is that bourgeois society is based on the crime of private property and that there is ultimately no difference between the burglar and the banker, apart from the fact that, as Polly points out in a wonderfully pithy monologue to the rest of the gang, the banker is better off because he is protected by society's laws.

The power of capitalism, for Marx, is its ability to hide the fact that it is based on exploitation. It appears to offer the worker a stable means of earning a living, when all it is doing is turning the worker into its slave. The tension between appearances and reality, which is at the heart of Marxist philosophy, runs throughout Pabst's film. As the street performer tells us in his song, the shark's teeth are never on show, just as the dandified appearance of Mackie belies the viciousness of his crimes, or the sugar-drenched soppiness of Polly and her husband's scenes together hides the fact that their marriage is a ruthless business arrangement which eventually brings the heads of the city's two main crime families together. The poor, the people who have the least to gain under capitalism, simply fall for the trick that their rulers play on them. At the end of the film, the beggars run out of control, hinting at the power of the proletariat and their revolutionary potential to change society. But rather than suggesting that this potential will one day be realised we see Peachum, their boss, go into partnership with big business to manipulate his people more effectively.

Verdict: Visually this is great. It's probably not fair to compare this too closely with Brecht's play. Film is, after all, a different medium but for me Pabst should have included more of Weill's songs. 3/5

M—Eine Stadt sucht einen Mörder/M (1931)

Cast: Peter Lorre (Hans Beckert), Gustaf Gründgens (Schraenker), Ellen Widmann (Madame Beckmann), Inge Landgut (Elsie Beckmann), Otto Wernicke (Inspector Karl Lohmann), Franz Stein (Minister), Theodor Loos (Police Commissioner Groeber), Friedrich Gnaß (Franz the Burglar), Fritz Odemar (Dynamiter), Paul Kemp (Pickpocket with 6 Watches), Theo Lingen (Bauernfaenger), Georg John (Blind Beggar), Karl Platen (Nightwatch), Gerhard Bienert (Secretary), Rosa Valetti (Elisabeth Winkler, Beckert's Landlady), Hertha von Walther (Prostitute), Ernst Stahl-Nachbaur (Police Chief), Rudolf Blümner (Beckert's Barrister), Lotte Loebinger (Isenta), Leonard Steckel (Karchow), Edgar Pauly (Kepich), Günter Neumann (Krehan)

Crew: Director Fritz Lang, Writers Fritz Lang and Thea von Harbou, Producer Seymour Nebenzal, Music Edvard Grieg (from *Peer Gynt*), Cinematography Fritz Arno Wagner, Production Design Emil Hasler and Karl Vollbrecht, Nero Film

Story: A distraught mother shouts from the balcony of her tenement building at a group of children who are singing a nursery rhyme about the bogeyman coming to chop them up. The reason for this overreaction soon becomes clear. The town is in the grip of a child-murdering serial killer. "Let them sing," says another woman. As long as they are singing the women at least know their children are safe. Little does this mother know that her own daughter, Elsie, is far from safe and that she has been picked up by the murderer. The mother waits for her daughter to return from school. As time goes on she becomes more and more frantic, screaming her daughter's name from the window of her flat, but to no avail. Elsie is already dead.

Hysteria seizes the town as the police work day and night to track down the killer, using all the forensic technology at their disposal to analyse clues left by the man. At the same time they are clamping down heavily on the activities of the underworld. This development doesn't go down well with the town's underworld bosses, who decide to take matters into their own hands and organise a search for the killer, enlisting the help of the town's beggar population who act as scouts.

Meanwhile the police net is closing in on the murderer whom they have now identified as Hans Beckert, a former patient in a lunatic asylum. But before the police manage to act on their information a blind beggar identifies Beckert from his whistle. This was the same tune he had heard a man with a child whistle just before the murder of Elsie. Now the same man is with a different child. Word is dispatched to the underworld and to prevent the man escaping before they can organise, one of their number slaps a large chalk 'M' on his coat so that he can be easily identified. As Beckert leads his next victim off he notices the 'M' on his coat in a shop window. Panic stricken he runs off, hiding from his underworld pursuers in an office building. That night the criminals break into the building and drag Beckert off to a deserted factory, where they have set up a kangaroo court. But before they lynch the man the police turn up, having discovered what is afoot, and take Beckert off for a legal trial.

Background: The story that Lang always told about *M* was that originally it was to be called *Murderers Amongst Us* but when he tried to hire the Staakan studios to start shooting he found himself refused access. He found this difficult to understand. He asked the studio manager why he wasn't allowed to make a film about a child killer. Realising for the first time what the film was about, the manager now beamed with relief and handed over his studio. Apparently the man, a member of the Nazi party, thought that the film was about Hitler and co. Child murderers were fine.

This was Lang's penultimate film before he left for Hollywood, and clearly foreshadows his future work. Visually we see a turn towards realism in his *mise en scène*, although we still see moments of abstract Expressionism, such as when the murderer Beckert is framed in a shop window by a diamond-shaped display of knives. Here the external world is used to reflect the internal thoughts of the character. *M* was Lang's first talkie and it is the use of sound which is most impressive about the film. As Eisner puts it, 'Sound is a central dramatic element, never additional or accidental, never an afterthought, but the counterpoint and supplement of the image.' If we look at the sequence when Elsie's mother realises that something is wrong with her daughter, we see the woman lean out the window calling Elsie's name. The sound of the woman's voice continues to be heard, ever more faintly, as the film cuts to a shot of the empty stairwell, followed by a shot of an empty laundry room, then to a shot of Elsie's empty dinner plate and finally to the ball Elsie was carrying when she was picked up. The sound of the woman's voice thus gives meaning to this montage of peopleless shots. Another famous moment when sound is used to construct the film's message is the sequence in which both the police and the underworld are planning how they are going to catch Beckert. As the film cuts between the meetings of the two organisations, the conversation from one seems to continue in the other, constructing each as the mirror image of the other and thus suggesting a degree of equivalence between these two apparently enemy worlds.

Subtext: One of the keys to the film's success is the incredible performance of Peter Lorre as Beckert. Lorre, who would later gain international fame by working with Humphrey Bogart in *Films Noirs* of the 1940s and 50s, perfectly portrays Beckert's schizophrenic personality which is half respectable member of society and half deranged killer. Beckert's character is built slowly through the film. Initially we don't even see him. Instead we are given a *Nosferatuesque* glimpse of his shadow, which is cast over a reward poster for his capture whilst, off screen we hear him talking to Elsie. (The connection with the earlier film is not surprising because they share the same cameraman.)

At the start of the film Beckert is a shadowy, evil monster, or as Kracauer puts it, an updated Cesare, who similarly lives with a compulsion to kill but who has no Caligari to control him. Yet, by the end of the film we have built up a far more three-dimensional psychological profile of a murderer than we get in Wiene's film. As Lang claimed, one of his reasons for making *M* was to try and understand what makes someone a murderer. In the kangaroo court sequence at the end of the film, the spectator, like the members of the underworld, is baying for Beckert's blood. The chief prosecutor puts his cards on the table: "You must be made safe. You must be got rid of!" but before he can act on his threats Beckert screams at the man "Can I help it? Can I help it?" Over the next few minutes Lorre then brilliantly changes our perception of Beckert from that of an evil monster into a victim of mental illness. He collapses to the floor, his wild eyes staring around the courtroom, as he vividly describes his feelings of paranoia. "Haven't I got this curse inside me... Again and again I have to walk the streets. And I always feel that somebody is following me... It is myself!" We are repulsed by Beckert as he thrashes around the courtroom like a trapped animal. We are disgusted by his rat-like features, his whining voice and above all his crimes. Yet at the same time we are forced to find some sympathy for him.

At the heart of the film is the question of how society should respond to crime. Lang deliberately parallels the worlds of the police and the criminals seeming to construct them both as equivalently important organisations of social order. But why do the criminals come together? Because business is bad. Moral action is contingent on the needs of capitalism. Beckert must be got rid of because he is undermining the normal equilibrium in society between the law and the criminal classes.

Crucially, the end of the film is left open. Beckert has escaped the rough justice of the kangaroo court but we are never told the outcome of the legal trial. In the final shot of the film we see Elsie's mother, one of the three women dressed in black, declaring that condemning Beckert will not bring her child back. Is the film's final message one of mercy, that society must treat the Beckerts of the world as people who are sick rather than as criminals?

Verdict: Probably Lang's finest film and the performance of Lorre's career. 5/5

Resource Materials

Filmography

This is an alphabetical list of all the major films produced in Germany between 1913 and 1933, from when film really got going in Germany until the takeover by the Nazis. The films that I've marked with an * are the ones that are generally seen as being part of the 'high' Expressionist period (1919-1927)

Abwege/Crisis (1928), d. G.W. Pabst

Abschied/Adieu (1930), d. Robert Siodmak

Algol (1920), d. Hans Werkmeister*

Alraune/Mandrake (1928), d. Henrik Galeen

Alraune/Mandrake (1930), d. Richard Oswald

Das Alte Gesetz/The Ancient Law (1923), d. E.A. Dupont

Anna Boleyn (1920), d. Ernst Lubitsch

Anna und Elisabeth (1933), d. Frank Wysbar

Ariana (1931), d. Paul Czinner

Asphalt (1929), d. Joe May

Atlantic (1920), d. E.A. Dupont

Berlin-Alexanderplatz (1931), d. Piel Jutzi

Berlin, die Symphonie der Grosstadt/Berlin, Symphony Of A City (1927), d. Walther Ruttmann

Der Blaue Engel/The Blue Angel (1930), d. Josef von Sternberg

Das Blaue Licht/The Blue Light (1932), d. Leni Riefenstahl

Der Brennende Acker/The Burning Earth (1922), d. F.W. Murnau

Die Büchse der Pandora/Pandora's Box (1928), d. G.W. Pabst

Die Buddenbrooks (1923), d. Gerhard Lamprecht

Das Cabinet des Dr Caligari/The Cabinet Of Dr Caligari (1919), d. Robert Wiene*

Carlos und Elisabeth (1924), d. Richard Oswald

Zur Chronik von Grieshuus/The Chronicles Of The Grey House (1925), d. Artur von Gerlach*

Danton (1921), d. Dimitri Buchowetzki

Dirnentragödie/Tragedy Of A Street (1927), d. Bruno Rahm

Dr Mabuse der Spieler/Dr Mabuse The Gambler (1922), d. Fritz Lang*

Die Dreigroschenoper/The Threepenny Opera (1931), d. G.W. Pabst

Emil und die Detektive/Emil And The Detectives (1931), d. Gerhard Lamprecht

Erdgeist/Earth Spirit (1923), d. Leopold Jessner*

Faust (1926), d. F.W. Murnau*

Die Frau im Mond/The Woman On The Moon (1929), d. Fritz Lang

Die freudlose Gasse/The Joyless Street (1925), d. G.W. Pabst

Geheimnisse einer Seele/Secrets Of A Soul (1926), d. G.W. Pabst

Genuine (1920), d. Robert Wiene*

Der Golem (1914), d. Paul Wegener, Henrik Galeen

Der Golem: Wie er in die Welt kam/The Golem: How He Came Into The World (1920), d. Paul Wegener, Carl Boese*

Die Haus ohne Tür/The House Without A Door (1914), d. Stellan Rye

Der Haus zum Mond/The House On The Moon (1921), d. Karl Heinz Martin*

Heimkehr/Homecoming (1928), d. Joe May

Die Herrin von Atlantis/The Mistress From Atlantis (1932), d. G.W. Pabst

Hintertreppe/Backstairs (1931), d. Leopold Jessner, Paul Leni

Homunculus (1916), d. Otto Rippert

Das Indische Grabmal/The Indian Tomb (1921), d. Joe May

I.N.R.I (1923), d. Robert Wiene

Jenseits der Strasse/Harbour Drift (1929), d. Leo Mittler

Das Cabinett des Dr Caligari/The Cabinet Of Dr Caligari (1919), d. Robert Wiene

Kameradschaft/Comradeship (1931), d. G.W. Pabst

Der Kongress tanzt/The Congress Dances (1931), d. Erich Charell

Kuhle Wampe/Whither Germany? (1932), d. Slatan Dudow

Der letzte Mann/The Last Laugh (1924), d. F.W. Murnau

Die Liebe der Jeanne Ney/The Love Of Jeanne Ney (1927), d. G.W. Pabst

Lukrezia Borgis (1922), d. Richard Oswald

M: Die Stadt sucht einen Mörder/M (1931), d. Fritz Lang

Madame Dubarry (1919), d. Ernst Lubitsch

Mädchen in Uniform/Girls In Uniform (1931), d. Leontine Sagen

Der Mann, der den Mord beging/The Man Who Murdered (1931), d. Kurt Bernhardt

Manon Lescaut (1926), d. Artur Robison

Der Melodie der Welt/World Melody (1929), d. Walter Ruttmann

Menschen am Sonntag/People On Sunday (1929), d. Robert Siodmak, Edgar Ulmer

Metropolis (1926), d. Fritz Lang*

Monna Vanna (1922), d. Richard Eichberg

Der Müde Tod/Destiny (1921), d. Fritz Lang*

Mutter Krausens Fahrt ins Glück/Mother Krausen's Journey Into Happiness (1929), d. Piel Jutzi

Mutter und Kind/Mother And Child (1924), d. Carl Froelich

Narkose/Narcosis (1929), d. Alfred Abel

*Die Nibelungen**
    Part One: *Siegfried* (1924), d. Fritz Lang
    Part Two: *Kriemhilds Rache/Kriemhild's Revenge* (1924), d. Fritz Lang

Nju (1924), d. Paul Czinner

Nosferatu, eine Symphonie des Grauens/Nosferatu, A Symphony Of Horror (1922), d. F.W. Murnau*

Orlacs Hände/The Hands Of Orlac (1924), d. Robert Wiene*

Othello (1922), d. Dimitri Buchowetzki

Peter der Grosse/Peter The Great (1923), d. Dimitri Buchowetzki

Phantom (1922), d. F.W. Murnau

Raskolnikov (1923), d. Robert Wiene*

Der Rattenfänger von Hameln/The Pied Piper Of Hamelin (1918), d. Paul Wegener

Rosenmontag/Rose Monday (1930), d. Hans Steinhoff

Schatten/Warning Shadows (1923), d. Artur Robison*

Der Schatz/The Treasure (1923), d. G.W. Pabst

Scherben/Shattered Fragments (1921), d. Lupu Pick

So ist das Leben/Such Is Life (1929), d. Carl Junghans

Die Spinnen (1919), d. Fritz Lang

Spione/Spies (1928), d. Fritz Lang

Der steinere Reiter / The Stone Rider (1923), d. Fritz Wendhausen*

Die Strasse/The Street (1923), d. Karl Grune

Der Student von Prag/The Student Of Prague (1913), d. Stellen Rye

Der Student von Prag/The Student Of Prague (1926), d. Henrik Galeen

Sumurun (1920), d. Ernst Lubitsch

Sylvester/New Year's Eve (1923), d. Lupu Pick

Tagebuch einer Verlorenen/Diary Of A Lost Girl (1929), d. G.W. Pabst

Tartüff/Tartuffe (1925), d. F.W. Murnau*

Das Testament des Dr Mabuse/The Testament Of Dr Mabuse (1933), d. Fritz Lang

Torgus (1920), d. Hans Kobe

Der träumende Mund/The Dreaming Mouth (1932), d. Paul Czinner

Überfall/Attack (1928), d. Ernö Metzner

Ungarische Rhapsodie/Hungarian Rhapsody (1928), Hanns Schwarz

Vanina (1922), d. Artur von Gerlach

Varieté/Variety (1925), d. E.A. Dupont

Der Verlorne Schuh/Cinderella (1923), d. Ludwig Berger

Von Morgens bis Mitternachts/From Morn To Midnight (1920), d. Karl
  Heinz Martin
Das Wachsfigurenkabinett/Waxworks (1924), d. Paul Leni*
Die Weber/The Weavers (1927), d. Friedrich Zelnik
Das Weib des Pharo/Pharaoh's Wife (1921), d. Ernst Lubitsch
Die Weisse Hölle von Piz Palü/The White Hell of Piz Palu (1929), d. Arnold
  Franck, G.W. Pabst
Westfront 1918 (1930), d. G.W. Pabst

Books and Articles

There is a huge amount of material available on German Expressionist
Film. Below I've listed all the sources I've used (including some in German), plus some other good starting points for those who want to find out
more.

General Books

Bordwell, David and Kristen Thompson, *Film History: An Introduction*
  (New York, 1994)
Coates, Paul, *The Gorgons Gaze: German Cinema, Expressionism, And The
  Image Of Horror* (Cambridge, 1991)
Cook, David, *A History Of Narrative Film*, 2nd edn. (New York, 1990)
Eisner, Lotte, *The Haunted Screen* (Berkeley, 1973)
Ellis, Jack C., *A History Of Film* (London, 1978)
Elsaesser, Thomas, *Weimar Cinema And After* (London, 2000)
Gay, Peter, *Weimar Culture: The Outsider As Insider* (London, 1974)
Jacobsen, W and Anton Kaes (eds), *Geschichte des deutschen Films* (Stut-
  tgart, 1993)
Kracauer, Siegfried, *From Caligari To Hitler* (Princeton, 1947)
Kreimeier. Klaus, *The Ufa Story. A History Of Germany's Greatest Film
  Company, 1918-1945* (Berkeley, 1999)
Kuzniar, Alice A., *The Queer German Cinema* (Stanford, 2000)
Lee, Stephen. J., *The Weimar Republic* (London, 1998)
Manvell, Roger and Heinrich Fraenkel, *The German Cinema* (London,
  1971)
Petro, P., *Joyless Streets: Women And Melodramatic Representation In
  Weimar Germany* (Princeton, 1989)
Salt, Barry, 'From Caligari to Who?,' *Sight and Sound* 48 (1970), 119-123
Sandford, John, `Chaos and Control in the Weimar Film,' *German Life and
  Letters*, 48 (1995), pp 311-23

On *Caligari* and Wiene

Budd, Mike (ed), *The Cabinet Of Dr Caligari. Texts, Contexts, Histories* (New Brunswick, 1990)

Carter, David R., 'Was There Such a Thing as Expressionist Cinema?' in Richard Sheppard (ed) *Expressionism In Focus. Proceedings Of The First UEA Symposium On German Studies* (Blairgowrie, 1987)

Kaes, Anton, 'The Expressionist Vision in Theater and Cinema' in Gertrud Bauer Picker and Karl Eugene Webb (eds), *Expressionism Reconsidered: Relationships And Affinities* (Munich, 1979), pp 89-98.

Minden, Michael, 'Politics and the silent cinema: The Cabinet of Dr Caligari and Battleship Potemkin' in Edward Timms and Peter Collier (eds), *Visions And Blueprints. Avant-Garde Culture And Radical Politics In Early Twentieth Century Europe* (Manchester, 1988)

Murphy, Richard J., 'Carnival Desire and the Sideshow of Fantasy: Dream, Duplicity and Representational Instability in The Cabinet of Dr Caligari,' *The Germanic Review* 66 (1991), pp 48-56

Prawer, Siegbert Solomon, *Caligari's Children: The Film As Tale Of Terror* (New York, 1980)

Robinson, David, *Das Cabinet des Dr Caligari* (London, 1997)

Rubenstein, Lenny, 'Caligari and the Rise of Expressionist Film' in Stephen Eric Bronner and Douglas Kellner (eds), *Passion And Rebellion: The Expressionist Heritage* (London, 1983)

On Lang

Bergstrom, Janet, 'Psychological Explanation in the Films of Lang and Pabst' in E Ann Kaplan (ed) *Psychoanalysis And Cinema* (New York, 1990)

Eisner, Lotte, *Fritz Lang* (London, 1976)

Gunning, Tom, *The Films Of Fritz Lang : Allegories Of Vision And Modernity* (London, 2000)

Jenkins, Stephen (ed), *Fritz Lang: The Image And The Look* (London, 1981)

Jensen, Paul M., *The Cinema Of Fritz Lang* (New York, 1969)

McGilligan, Patrick, *Fritz Lang: The Nature Of The Beast* (London, 1997)

Rutsky, R.L., 'The Mediation of Technology and Gender: Metropolis, Nazism, Modernism,' *New German Critique* 60 (1993), pp 3-32

On Pabst and Brooks

Bergstrom, Janet, 'Psychological Explanation in the Films of Lang and Pabst' in E Ann Kaplan (ed) *Psychoanalysis And Cinema* (New York, 1990)

Brooks, Louise, *Lulu In Hollywood* (London, 1982)

Doane, Mary Ann, 'The Erotic Barter: Pandora's Box,' in Doane, Mary Ann (ed), *Femmes Fatales: Feminism, Film Theory, Psychoanalysis* (New York, 1991)

Lamb, Stephen, 'Woman's nature? Images of women in The Blue Angel, Pandora's Box, Kuhle Wampe and Girls in Uniform' in Marsha Meskimmon and Shearer West (eds) *Visions Of The 'Neue Frau': Women And The Visual Arts In Weimar Germany* (Aldershot, 1995)

Rentschler, Eric (ed) *The Films Of G.W. Pabst: An Extraterritorial Cinema* (New Brunswick, 1990) - most of the references to critics come from this collection of articles

On Murnau

Collier, Jo Leslie, *From Wagner To Murnau. The Transposition Of Romanticism From Stage To Screen* (London, 1998)

Eisner, Lotte, *F.W. Murnau* (London, 1964)

Prodolliet, Ernest, *Nosferatu. die Entwicklung des Vampirfilms von Friedrich Wilhelm Murnau bis Werner Herzog* (Freiburg, 1980)

On Sternberg and Dietrich

Baxter, Peter (ed), *Sternberg* (London, 1980)

Lamb, Stephen, 'Woman's nature? Images of women in The Blue Angel, Pandora's Box, Kuhle Wampe and Girls in Uniform' in Marsha Meskimmon and Shearer West (eds) *Visions Of The 'Neue Frau': Women And The Visual Arts In Weimar Germany* (Aldershot, 1995)

Studlar, Gaylyn, *In The Realm Of Pleasure Von Sternberg, Dietrich, And The Masochistic Aesthetic* (New York, 1992)

Bogdanovich, Peter, *Who The Devil Made It* (New York, 1997)

Von Sternberg, Josef, *Fun In A Chinese Laundry* (London Columbus, 1987)

The Web

Again, there is a huge amount of material on the web. A good place to start for most films is of course International Movie Database: www.imdb.com.

A lot of the really good sites on Expressionism are in German but they are still worth having a look at for their picture archives if you can't read the language. There are three good general German film sites with sizeable chunks devoted to Expressionism: www.dasfilmarchiv.de; www.cine-graph.de; www.deutsches-filminstitut.de

Kinoeye is a good online film journal which has lots of interesting stuff in its archive about Expressionism: www.kinoeye.org

A good site on silent movies in general is: www.silent-movies.com

Finally, here's a link to an online museum with lots of information about Expressionism as well as its cultural context: www.dhm.de/lemo/home.html

If you want to find out about some of the directors and stars that I've looked at in this book, try these sites:

For Louise Brooks: www.pandorasbox.com
For Marlene Dietrich: www.marlene.com
For Fritz Lang: www.bfi.org.uk/features/lang/
For F.W. Murnau: www.sloppyfilms.com/murnau/index.html
For G.W. Pabst: www.geocities.com/louisebrookssociety/pabst-links.html
For Josef von Sternberg: www.mdle.com/ClassicFilms/BTC/direct21.htm

The Essential Library: Best-Sellers

Build up your library with new titles every month

Film Noir by Paul Duncan

The laconic private eye, the corrupt cop, the heist that goes wrong, the femme fatale with the rich husband and the dim lover - these are the trademark characters of Film Noir. This book charts the progression of the Noir style as a vehicle for film-makers who wanted to record the darkness at the heart of American society as it emerged from World War to the Cold War. As well as an introduction explaining the origins of Film Noir, seven films are examined in detail and an exhaustive list of over 500 Films Noirs are listed.

Alfred Hitchcock by Paul Duncan

More than 20 years after his death, Alfred Hitchcock is still a household name, most people in the Western world have seen at least one of his films, and he popularised the action movie format we see every week on the cinema screen. He was both a great artist and dynamite at the box office. This book examines the genius and enduring popularity of one of the most influential figures in the history of the cinema!

Orson Welles by Martin Fitzgerald

The popular myth is that after the artistic success of *Citizen Kane* it all went downhill for Orson Welles, that he was some kind of fallen genius. Yet, despite overwhelming odds, he went on to make great Films Noirs like *The Lady From Shanghai* and *Touch Of Evil*. He translated Shakespeare's work into films with heart and soul (*Othello, Chimes At Midnight, Macbeth*), and he gave voice to bitterness, regret and desperation in *The Magnificent Ambersons* and *The Trial*. Far from being down and out, Welles became one of the first cutting-edge independent film-makers.

Woody Allen (Revised & Updated Edition) by Martin Fitzgerald

Woody Allen: Neurotic. Jewish. Funny. Inept. Loser. A man with problems. Or so you would think from the characters he plays in his movies. But hold on. Allen has written and directed 30 films. He may be a funny man, but he is also one of the most serious American film-makers of his generation. This revised and updated edition includes *Sweet And Lowdown* and *Small Time Crooks*.

Stanley Kubrick by Paul Duncan

Kubrick's work, like all masterpieces, has a timeless quality. His vision is so complete, the detail so meticulous, that you believe you are in a three-dimensional space displayed on a two-dimensional screen. He was commercially successful because he embraced traditional genres like War (*Paths Of Glory, Full Metal Jacket*), Crime (*The Killing*), Science Fiction (*2001*), Horror (*The Shining*) and Love (*Barry Lyndon*). At the same time, he stretched the boundaries of film with controversial themes: underage sex (*Lolita*); ultra violence (*A Clockwork Orange*); and erotica (*Eyes Wide Shut*).

The Essential Library: Recent Releases

Build up your library with new titles every month

Tim Burton by Colin Odell & Michelle Le Blanc

Tim Burton makes films about outsiders on the periphery of society. His heroes are psychologically scarred, perpetually naive and childlike, misunderstood or unintentionally disruptive. They upset convential society and morality. Even his villains are rarely without merit - circumstance blurs the divide between moral fortitude and personal action. But most of all, his films have an aura of the fairytale, the fantastical and the magical.

French New Wave by Chris Wiegand

The directors of the French New Wave were the original film geeks - a collection of celluloid-crazed cinéphiles with a background in film criticism and a love for American auteurs. Having spent countless hours slumped in Parisian cinémathèques, they armed themselves with handheld cameras, rejected conventions, and successfully moved movies out of the studios and on to the streets at the end of the 1950s.

Borrowing liberally from the varied traditions of film noir, musicals and science fiction, they released a string of innovative and influential pictures, including the classics *Jules Et Jim* and *A Bout De Souffle.* By the mid-1960s, the likes of Jean-Luc Godard, François Truffaut, Claude Chabrol, Louis Malle, Eric Rohmer and Alain Resnais had changed the rules of film-making forever.

Bollywood by Ashok Banker

Bombay's prolific Hindi-language film industry is more than just a giant entertainment juggernaut for 1 billion-plus Indians worldwide. It's a part of Indian culture, language, fashion and lifestyle. It's also a great bundle of contradictions and contrasts, like India itself. Thrillers, horror, murder mysteries, courtroom dramas, Hong Kong-style action gunfests, romantic comedies, soap operas, mythological costume dramas... they're all blended with surprising skill into the musical boy-meets-girl formula of Bollywood. This vivid introduction to Bollywood, written by a Bollywood scriptwriter and media commentator, examines 50 major films in entertaining and intimate detail.

Mike Hodges by Mark Adams

Features an extensive interview with Mike Hodges. His first film, *Get Carter*, has achieved cult status (recently voted the best British film ever in *Hotdog* magazine) and continues to be the benchmark by which every British crime film is measured. His latest film, *Croupier*, was such a hit in the US that is was re-issued in the UK. His work includes crime drama (*Pulp*), science-fiction (*Flash Gordon* and *The Terminal Man*), comedy (*Morons From Outer Space*) and watchable oddities such as *A Prayer For The Dying* and *Black Rainbow*. Mike Hodges is one of the great maverick British filmmakers.

The Essential Library: Currently Available

Film Directors:

Woody Allen (2nd)	Tim Burton	Ang Lee
Jane Campion*	John Carpenter	Joel & Ethan Coen (2nd)
Jackie Chan	Steve Soderbergh	Clint Eastwood
David Cronenberg	Terry Gilliam*	Michael Mann
Alfred Hitchcock (2nd)	Krzysztof Kieslowski*	Roman Polanski
Stanley Kubrick (2nd)	Sergio Leone	Oliver Stone
David Lynch	Brian De Palma*	George Lucas
Sam Peckinpah*	Ridley Scott (2nd)	James Cameron
Orson Welles (2nd)	Billy Wilder	
Steven Spielberg	Mike Hodges	

Film Genres:

Blaxploitation Films	Bollywood	French New Wave
Horror Films	Spaghetti Westerns	Vietnam War Movies
Slasher Movies	Film Noir	German Expresionist Films
Vampire Films*	Heroic Bloodshed*	

Film Subjects:

Laurel & Hardy	Marx Brothers	Film Music
Steve McQueen*	Marilyn Monroe	The Oscars® (2nd)
Filming On A Microbudget	Bruce Lee	Writing A Screenplay

TV:

Doctor Who

Literature:

Cyberpunk	Philip K Dick	The Beat Generation
Agatha Christie	Sherlock Holmes	Noir Fiction*
Terry Pratchett	Hitchhiker's Guide (2nd)	Alan Moore
William Shakespeare		

Ideas:

Conspiracy Theories	Nietzsche	UFOs
Feminism	Freud & Psychoanalysis	Bisexuality

History:

Alchemy & Alchemists	The Crusades	The Black Death
Jack The Ripper	The Rise Of New Labour	Ancient Greece
American Civil War	American Indian Wars	

Miscellaneous:

The Madchester Scene	Stock Market Essentials	Beastie Boys
How To Succeed As A Sports Agent		
How To Succeed In The Music Business		

Available at all good bookstores or send a cheque (payable to 'Oldcastle Books') to: **Pocket Essentials (Dept GEF), 18 Coleswood Rd, Harpenden, Herts, AL5 1EQ, UK**. £3.99 each (£2.99 if marked with an *). For each book add 50p postage & packing in the UK and £1 elsewhere.